Guide to t

North American Ethnographic Collections

at the

University of Pennsylvania Museum of Archaeology and Anthropology

Guide to the
North American Ethnographic Collections
at the
University of Pennsylvania Museum of Archaeology and Anthropology

Lucy Fowler Williams

University of Pennsylvania Museum of Archaeology and Anthropology

Copyright © 2003 by
University of Pennsylvania Museum of Archaeology and Anthropology
3260 South Street, Philadelphia, Pennsylvania 19104

All Rights Reserved

First Edition

> *The Museum gratefully acknowledges that this publication was made possible in part through generous gifts to the Museum*
>
> *in memory of:*
>
> Melissa Freeman
> Elizabeth Peterson
> Virginia and Lee Philips
> Robert Trescher
>
> *and in honor of:*
>
> Penny and Robert Fox.

LIBRARY OF CONGRESS CATALOGING-IN-PUBLICATION DATA

University of Pennsylvania. Museum of Archaeology and Anthropology.
  Guide to the North American ethnographic collections at the University of Pennsylvania Museum of Archaeology and Anthropology / Lucy Fowler Williams.– 1st ed.
    p. cm.
  Includes bibliographical references and index.
  ISBN 1-931707-32-4 (alk. paper) – ISBN 1-931707-33-2 (pbk. : alk. paper)
  1. University of Pennsylvania. Museum of Archaeology and Anthropology–Guidebooks. 2. Indians of North America–Material culture–Catalogs.
  3. Indian art–North America–Catalogs. I. Williams, Lucy Fowler. II. Title.
  E76.85.U65 2003
  973.0497'0074'74811–dc21
                                    2003007172

Frontispiece: (from top, l. to r.) "Shotridge with dog sled on Chilkat River," photo by Louis Shotridge, March 1923 (neg. S5-14918); "Thomas N. in fur cap, leather beaded jacket," photo by Louis Shotridge, ca. 1925 (neg. S5-15165); "Winnebago, Chief Jasper," photo by Frank G. Speck, ca. 1920 (neg. S4-143938); "Daughter of Chief Symbestre (?), Montagnais-Naskapi, Saint Augustin Band," photo by Frank G. Speck, 1935 (neg. S4-143942); "Four Eskimo," photo by George Gordon, 1905–1907 (neg. S8-138916).

∞ Printed in Canada on acid-free paper.

Contents

Illustrations vii
Foreword, Robert W. Preucel xi
Acknowledgments xiii
Of Spirits and Science: Meaning and Material Culture
   Crossing Boundaries 1
      The North American Ethnographic Holdings 3
      The Edward Avery McIlhenny Collection 5
      The Stewart Culin Collection 6
      The George Byron Gordon Collection 8
      The Louis Shotridge Collection 11
      The Frank G. Speck Collection 13
      NAGPRA and Beyond 15
Readings 18
Plates 19
Appendix: Major North American Ethnographic Collections
   at the University of Pennsylvania Museum 92
Index 95
About the Author 98

Illustrations

Frontispiece ii

FIGURES
1. Map of North America xiv
2. The University Museum's American Gallery, ca. 1912 4
3. Stewart Culin, 1900 7
4. Zuni game tubes 8
5. George Gordon, 1905 9
6. "Five Native Alaskans," by George Gordon, 1905 9
7. "After the first snow, and no snowshoes," by Louis Shotridge, ca. 1918 11
8. "Two Tlingit Girls," by Louis Shotridge 12
9. Frank G. Speck with Cayuga informants 13
10. "Young Gerome," Montagnais-Naskapi, by Frank G. Speck 15

PLATES
1. Mask, Yup'ik 20
2. Hunting visor, Alaska 21
3. Bola, Iñupiaq 21
4. Bird charm, Yup'ik 22
5. Ceremonial gloves 22
6. Fishskin coat, Yup'ik 23
7. Cotton *atigluks*, Iñupiaq 23
8. Beaded inner parka (*atigi*), Iglulik 24
9. Hide outfit, Athapaskan 24
10. Modern Ingalik masks, by Raymond Dutchman 25
11. Dance masks of wild man, Ingalik 25
12. Coat with quillwork, Northern Athapaskan 26
13. Mittens, Ahtna 26

14.	Basket, Chilcotin	27
15.	Hunting coat, Innu (Naskapi)	28
16.	Shot pouches, Innu (Naskapi)	28
17.	Drag string, Innu (Naskapi)	29
18.	Divination bones, Innu (Naskapi)	29
19.	Beaded coat, Cree	30
20.	Saddle, Cree	31
21.	Artist's pattern set, Tlingit	31
22.	Hats, Kaagwaantaan clan, Tlingit	32–33
23.	Hats, Kaagwaantaan Drum House, Tlingit	32–33
24.	Eagle staff head, Tlingit	33
25.	House posts, Tlingit	34–35
26.	Grizzly bear tunic, Tlingit	36
27.	Frog tunic, Tlingit	36
28.	Octopus staff, Tlingit	37
29.	Food dish, Tlingit	37
30.	Heye collection of Northwest Coast items	38
31.	Copper, Tlingit	38
32.	Mask, Haida	39
33.	Silas Saunders, Nuxalt (Bella Coola)	40
34.	Horn bowl, Haida	40
35.	Evelyn Vanderhoop, Haida	41
36.	Button blanket by Haida artist Dorothy Grant	41
37a.	Hat by Charles and Isabella Edenshaw, Haida	42
37b.	Detail of Haida Edenshaw hat	42
38.	Chief Peo's beaded coat, Umatilla	43
39.	Twined bag, Plateau	44
40a.	Dress, Nez Perce	45
40b.	Detail of Nez Perce dress	45
41.	Twined basket, Skokomish	46
42.	Basket by Karuk weaver Elizabeth Hickox	46
43.	Feast bowl by Pomo weaver Sally Burris	47
44.	Pomo basket weaver Sally Burris	47
45a.	Dance skirt, Hupa	48
45b.	Detail, Hupa dance skirt	48
46.	Shawn Kane, Hupa	49

47.	Feathered basket, Pomo	50–51
48.	Baskets by Datsolalee, Washoe	50–51
49.	Shirt, Paiute	51
50.	Jar, Ashiwi polychrome	52
51.	Jar, Acoma Pueblo	53
52.	Shalako Mana katsina, Hopi	54
53.	Long Hair and Hu-tu-tu katsinas, Zuni Pueblo	54
54.	Serape, Navajo	55
55.	Hopi ring and dart game	56
56.	Arwen Nuttall, Louisiana Cherokee	56
57.	Shonto Begay, Navajo	57
58.	Jar by Dextra Quotskuyva Nampeyo	57
59.	Jar by Les Namingha	58
60.	Drum by Gabriel Trujillo, Cochiti Pueblo	58
61.	Woven garments, San Juan Pueblo	59
62.	Ramoncita Sandoval, Tewa	59
63.	"Nested Lives" by Roxanne Swentzell	60
64.	Man's buffalo robe, Lakota	60–61
65.	Woman's buffalo robe, Lakota	60–61
66.	Shirt, Pawnee	62
67.	Quilled shirt, Mandan, ca. 1830	62–63
68a.	Quilled leggings, Mandan, ca. 1830	62–63
68b.	Detail, Mandan leggings	62–63
69a.	Shirt worn by American Horse, Lakota	64
69b.	Detail of Lakota shirt	64
70.	Shirt, Crow	65
71.	Painting tools, Blackfeet	65
72.	Side fold dress, Northern Plains	66
73.	Beaded dress, Lakota	67
74.	Dress with silver brooch, Lakota	68
75.	Elk tooth dress, Crow	68
76.	Elk tooth	69
77.	Umbilical amulets, Lakota	69
78.	Child's dress, Cheyenne/Arapaho	70
79.	Bladder bags, Lakota	70
80.	Beaded bag panels, Lakota	71

81.	Donna Shakespear-Cummings, Northern Arapaho	72
82.	Ornament, Mandan-Hidatsa	72
83.	Necklace, Dakota	73
84.	Pipe stems collected by George Catlin	74
85.	Pipe bowl collected by George Catlin	74
86.	Feather box made by Powerful Cloud, Dakota	75
87.	Drum, Blackfeet	75
88.	Beaded sashes, Choctaw	76
89.	Choctaw Earnest Fauve, 1902	76
90.	Shirt, Eastern Cherokee	77
91.	Cherokee Chief, Will West Long, 1930s	77
92.	Shoulder bag, Shawnee	78
93.	Choctaw bag by Jerry Ingram	79
94.	Medicinal objects, Eastern Cherokee	80
95.	Beaver bowl, Kaskaskia	80
96.	Coat, Shawnee	81
97.	Beaded leggings, Ojibwa (?)	81
98.	Bandolier bag, Winnebago (?)	82
99.	Bandolier bag, Great Lakes region	82
100.	Beaded leggings, Menomini	83
101a.	Ceremonial club, Winnebago	84
101b.	Ceremonial club, Winnebago	84
102.	Woman's blouse, Delaware	85
103.	Delaware woman	85
104.	Beaded bags, Iroquois	86
105.	Moccasins, Iroquois	87
106.	Embroidered birchbark trays, Huron	87
107a.	Lacrosse stick, Cayuga	88–89
107b.	Detail, Lacrosse stick	88–89
107c.	Detail, Lacrosse stick	88–89
108.	Mohegan mask by Harold Tantaquidgeon	89
109.	Shoulder cape, Penobscot	90
110.	Clara Neptune, Penobscot, 1912	91

Foreword

The last half of the 19th century is popularly known as the Golden Age of museums in the United States. During this period, a number of museums were founded in whole or in part to house and exhibit the archaeological and ethnographic materials of Native Americans. Prominent among these were the Smithsonian Institution, founded in 1846; the Peabody Museum of Harvard University, founded in 1866; the American Museum of Natural History, founded in 1869; and the Field Museum of Natural History, founded in 1893. Fierce rivalries emerged between these museums as they struggled to acquire Native American objects.

The justification for this collecting activity was a complex intersection of moral, ethical, and pragmatic concerns. Anthropologists viewed material culture as a crucial source of data in illustrating the natural history of humankind. Although all humans were regarded as cognitively equivalent, Native American cultures were regarded as occupying a lower stage on the evolutionary ladder than those of the United States and Britain. In popular circles, Native American material culture was valued as part of a uniquely American history, something that set off and distinguished the New World from its Old World counterpart. At the same time, it seemed inevitable to many that Native Americans were "vanishing" and that salvage ethnographies were needed to insure against the loss of knowledge of their cultural accomplishments.

Although the University of Pennsylvania Museum of Archaeology and Palaeontology was founded in 1887 to focus upon the study of the civilizations of the ancient Near East, it was quick to incorporate the collecting of Native American material culture under the influence of Daniel Garrison Brinton, the first professor of anthropology in the United States. This program began on a modest scale with the archaeological work of Charles C. Abbott and Henry Chapman Mercer at Abbott's farm in Trenton, New Jersey, from 1889 to 1897 and Frank Hamilton Cushing at Key Marco, Florida, in 1896.

The collecting of contemporary Native American ethnographic materials was soon added. Between 1900 and 1929, numerous ethnographic collecting expeditions were sent to northern, western, and southeastern Alaska (Iñupiaq, Yupik, Ingalik, Tlingit), Arizona (Hopi), Delaware (Nanticoke), Labrador (Montagnais), Maine (Abenaki, Micmac, Passamaquoddy, Penobscot), New Brunswick (Malaseet, Micmac), North Dakota (Dakota), New Mexico (Isleta, Zuni), North Dakota (Dakota), Nova Scotia (Micmac), Oklahoma (Osage and Yuchi), Quebec (Montagnais), Utah (Ute and Paiute), and Virginia (Pamunkey and Mattapony). In addition to collecting material culture some of these expeditions documented native languages and songs.

As Lucy Fowler Williams, Keeper of Collections of the American Section, notes in her essay, systematic collections are extremely important from a scientific point of view. The collections made by scholars such as Edward McIlhenny, Stewart Culin, George Byron Gordon, Louis Shotridge, and Frank G. Speck go beyond the artifact as an aesthetic object to reveal the materiality of the histories and social practices of native peoples. Among these individuals, however, Louis Shotridge, a native Tlingit Indian from Klukwan, Alaska, stands out. His goals were to showcase his own people by placing important examples of their material culture alongside those of the great civilizations of the world, particularly Egypt, China, and the ancient Near East. Even though some Tlingit people today criticize him for his collecting activities, it is clear that had he not acquired these remarkable objects, many of them would have been destroyed.

Today, museums are reinterpreting their mission statements and responding to a host of new social and political concerns, foremost among which is their changing relationship with Native Americans. In addition to its efforts to comply with the Native American Graves Protection and Repatriation Act of 1990, the University Museum is actively working to develop collaborative exhibits with Native groups, to share its collections with Native artists and researchers, and to provide research opportunities for Native students.

ROBERT W. PREUCEL
Associate Curator of North America

Acknowledgments

The creation of this book has been a distinct pleasure thanks to the many people who have contributed to its production. I am most grateful to Robert W. Preucel, Associate Professor and Associate Curator of North America, whose thoughtful advice and ongoing support of this project have helped focus and guide it along the way.

Several other staff members of the Museum have contributed their time and knowledge. I thank Dr. Jeremy A. Sabloff, Williams Director, Chief Curator Robert Sharer and Associate Curator Clark Erickson of the American Section for their support and comments on final drafts. Also from the American Section Assistant Keeper William Wierzbowski provided valuable advice and assistance; Melissa Elsberry, former Native American Graves Project and Repatriation Act (NAGPRA) Project Coordinator, contributed comments and important suggestions; and I thank Stacey Espenlaub, NAGPRA Coordinator, for her skilled assistance in so many different ways. I am also grateful to Francine Sarin, Chief Photographer, and her Assistant, Jennifer Chiappardi, for their talent and patience throughout the process of photography; Alex Pezzati, Archivist, for his assistance in providing access to collections records and for sharing his breadth of knowledge about the history of the Museum; and Charles Kline, Photo Archivist, for access to images and assistance in their reproduction. Kevin Lamp of the Director's Office contributed his expertise in developing the map and drawing. From the Publications Department I am particularly grateful to Walda Metcalf, Assistant Director for Publications, who initially encouraged the development of a guide to the collections and whose resolve saw the project to completion; and to Jennifer Quick, Senior Editor, who skillfully designed the final product.

Several other individuals contributed their time and expertise and I am grateful to each of them—Shane Bernard, Historian and Curator of the McIlhenny Company, Louisiana; Carol Sandoval, Manager of the Oke Oweenge Craft Cooperative, San Juan Pueblo, New Mexico; Raymond Dutchman of Shageluk, Alaska; Bob Maguire of Fairbanks, Alaska; Nate Gilmore, Nate Rice, and Ted Daeschler of the Academy of Natural Sciences of Philadelphia; Robin Wright, Curator, Burke Museum, Seattle; and Felicia Pickering, National Museum of Natural History. I also thank Shonto Begay, Donna Shakespear-Cummings, Shawn Kane, Arwen Nuttall, Ramoncita Sandoval, Silas Saunders, and Evelyn Vanderhoop for permission to publish their photographs.

Finally, I would like to recognize and thank the past Keepers of the collection, particularly Pamela Jardine and Judith Berman, and the many volunteers who have, over the years, devoted so much of their time and energy to help care for and document these important records of American Indian life.

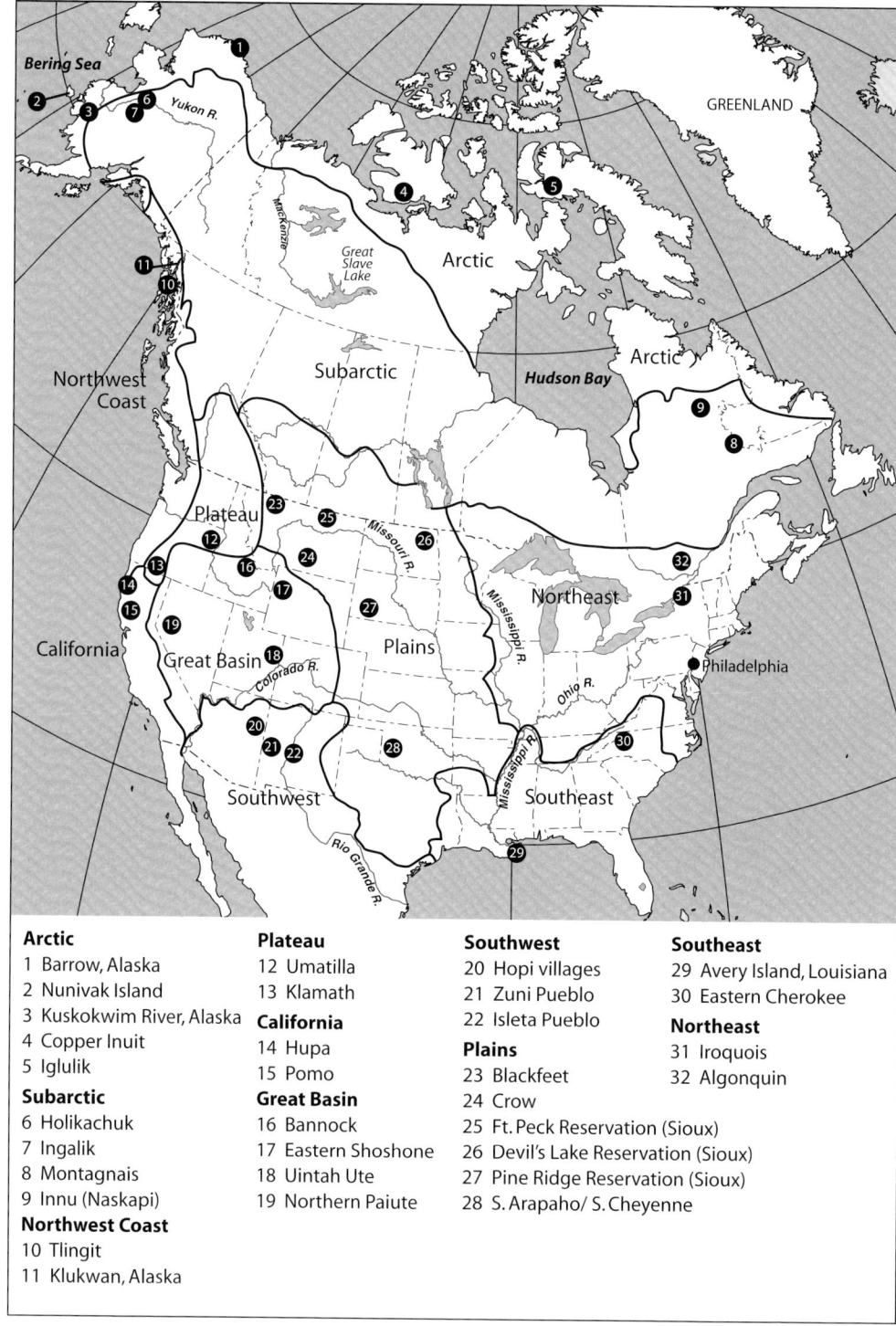

Figure 1. North American cultures and communities emphasized in the University of Pennsylvania Museum's ethnographic collections. Map by Kevin Lamp.

Of Spirits and Science: Meaning and Material Culture Crossing Boundaries

The North American ethnographic collections of the University of Pennsylvania Museum of Archaeology and Anthropology (UPM) contain nearly 40,000 objects from Canada, the United States, and the Caribbean which together document the remarkable diversity of past and present native peoples. The objects were acquired primarily between 1880 and 1940, when UPM actively laid the cornerstones of its collection. Although not all of these collections are displayed in the Museum's galleries, they are preserved and available for study in the Museum's Mainwaring Wing, a new artifact storage and study facility that opened in 2002. This Guide, which illustrates a mere fraction of the Native American holdings, is intended to offer both an introduction and an invitation to these collections.

The objects housed at the Museum tell thousands of different stories: of Lakota women who created traditional garments covered in lavish beadwork that incorporated protective symbols (Plate 73); of Inuit men who fashioned specialized hunting equipment that allowed them to endure the harsh Arctic environment (Plate 1); and of tribal leaders and spokesmen who traveled in their finery to Washington, DC (Plate 38). They also tell us what life was like on the reservations (Plate 80) and how it might have felt to be visited by an anthropologist or someone with enough of a calling to take them west of the Mississippi (Plate 8).

In addition, the collections hold information about the methods and motives of the collectors (Plates 3, 17, 22, 90) and the histories of the objects since coming to the Museum (Plates 25 and 56).

Such stories reveal that objects possess multiple meanings within different cultural contexts, and each of these meanings is culturally defined. A Tlingit Killer Whale hat, for example (Plate 22), made to honor an esteemed leader at a particular clan's Alaskan ceremonial feast, may have possessed a different meaning for its collector as an aesthetic artifact, and still different meanings for the Philadelphia Museum community where it was later displayed.

One of the goals of this Guide is to illustrate objects in the collection that are well documented. Since the Museum is devoted to the study of the social, cultural, and biological history of the human species, documentation that ties objects to a particular native person, place, and time provides a deeper understanding of the roles those objects played within their own communities (Plates 23, 42, 107). Though many of these native names may be unfamiliar, their presence allows us to imagine the objects being made, used, and cared for and enables us in the 21st century to relate to the past more directly.

The objects illustrated also reflect the goals of the collectors who, with vision and specific motives, acquired Native American objects and in the process helped preserve the medium of American Indian material culture during times of social and political change. Famous names such as Meriwether Lewis and William Clark, George Catlin, John Wesley Powell, Frank Hamilton Cushing, and George Heye are among those associated with the Museum's American collections. But there are also many less familiar names—such as Frederica de Laguna, Louis Shotridge, Edward Avery McIlhenny, and Thomas Donaldson—belonging to anthropologists, Native Americans, naturalists, government agents, artists and journalists, each with a different story and background. What were these collectors' goals? And how did they interact with the native peoples whose things they collected? How did they choose the particular items they collected? This Guide tells some of these interesting stories as well.

Unlike the literate traditions of Europe, which have been documented by generations of written texts, the teachings of Native North Americans are played out in oral and material traditions that communicate life's experience between and across generations. As a result, an important record of Native American philosophy is the objects themselves. These objects can tell us about the ways in which Native Americans experience their worlds and how they interact with and depend on objects to make their lives meaningful. Many objects continue to be sources of knowledge and inspiration for native peoples today.

For native people of past and present generations, knowledge is derived from and revealed through the spirit world and lived experience. Among the Innu (Naskapi) in Labrador, for example, a sunbeam breaking through the clouds signifies a blessing and directional instruction to a hunter in search of caribou; for the Hopi of Arizona, rain falling on the desert signifies renewal and a blessing from the Hopi spirits; or for the Inuit of Alaska, the image of a particular animal is dreamed and received as a gift from the spirit world for guidance in the physical world. These experiences are often given expression in objects using a visual language of material symbols. As a result, the meanings of objects often represent personal experiences of the maker with the spiritual world. Though sometimes these symbols are explicit and seemingly easy to read, such as a depiction of a buffalo (Plate 87) or a bear painted on a hide shirt (Plate 26), their contextualized meanings are often multivalent and best understood by the individual maker or within that maker's society. This Guide provides a combination of native and non-native interpretations of such imagery.

The arrival of Europeans in North America late in the 15th century heralded a profound change in Native American material culture. Europeans and, later, Euro-Americans offered trade goods and cash for Indian curios. Many talented native artists began to tailor some of their creations to satisfy the demands of outsiders (Plates 48 and 106). In the process, objects that in their native contexts may have represented spiritual knowledge and lived experience were purchased and brought to Philadelphia where their original significance was often transformed into ethnic markers of particular tribal groups in cultural decline. Regardless of the effects of colonialism, the adoption of new materials such as glass beads, machined trade cloth, or commercial paints was guided by native principles which are often still evident in Native American material culture. Making choices to accept or reject new materials, Native people have remained skilled and creative artisans, adapting diverse resources to suit their changing needs in new and unique ways (Plate 102).

The majority of the Museum's Native American ethnographic collections were acquired at a time when it was generally understood that American Indian culture was coming to an abrupt end. By 1880, Indians had already experienced three centuries of confrontation with Europeans and Euro-Americans, whose interests in westward expansion fueled a relentless determination to dominate and "civilize" the Indian tribes. Once warfare and introduced diseases had taken their toll, tribal leaders had little choice but to surrender to the U.S. government and accept life on reservation lands as a matter of their very survival. It is within this context of change and high mortality rates that the notion of the "vanishing" Indian provoked both popular and scientific interest in salvaging Indian heritage. Beginning with the Philadelphia Centennial Exposition of 1876, American Indian objects were systematically sought out and displayed in museums as authentic traits or facts representing particular Indian tribes before contact. Tools, pottery, weapons, and clothing illustrating all aspects of Indian life and tribes were routinely displayed in museums across America.

At this same time, the discipline of anthropology was establishing itself as the science of humankind, and the study of Native Americans served as a central focus for scholars in the United States and elsewhere. For the first three quarters of the 19th century, anthropologists studied the languages, physical characteristics, and archaeology of indigenous American peoples. Scholars were interested in the questions of the age of the human race, the peopling of the Americas, and the progress of humanity or civilization in a particular area. Ethnology, the comparative study of living cultures, was of interest to the degree that it could shed light on those larger questions. Within an evolutionary framework that viewed human societies as representing stages of human development along a continuum from savagery to civilization, contemporary material culture was one ready means of graphically illustrating human development. By the first quarter of the 20th century, under the influence of Franz Boas, anthropologists began to move away from evolutionary models and a strong interest developed in historical studies. But by the middle of the century, the focus on Native American objects, customs and beliefs began to wane in favor of a larger project that viewed world social, economic, and political interaction as a potential field of study.

The University Museum's beginnings and the origins of the University's Anthropology Department took place during these periods. The Museum was formally established in 1887, and the American Section was led by the renowned anthropologist Daniel G. Brinton. Brinton embodied many of the characteristics of the early evolutionary-oriented scientists and sought to systematically document native languages and literature. With the appointment of archaeologist Charles C. Abbott as Curator in 1890, research began on the antiquity of humans in the Delaware Valley. Later Curator and Director George Gordon actively promoted academic anthropology at the Museum by teaching unoffical anthropology courses. In 1911 he and Frank G. Speck were instrumental in establishing a formal teaching Department of Anthropology at Penn. Speck, more than Gordon, was an exemplar of the historical approach of Boas, having studied with him at Columbia.

The North American Ethnographic Holdings

The Museum's ethnographic holdings from North America are the results of thirty ethnological collecting expeditions and thousands of donations (see Appendix). Unlike most art museums, this collection includes a vast array of objects of everyday life, the belongings of elders, men, women, and children. What kinds of objects are housed here? Fishing and hunting equipment (Plates 3 and 17), clothing (Plates 6-9, 27, 49, 66-70, 72-75, 100), and weapons, tools, and feast dishes (Plates 29, 34, 91); saddles (Plate 20), snowshoes, knives and pipes (Plates 84 and 85), musical instruments and hairbrushes; tweezers, ornaments, lip plugs, and medicines; toys and games (Plate 55), house models, dolls, and baby carriers; items used in ritual and ceremony (Plates 45, 101), raw materials, even totem poles and canoes.

Figure 2. The University Museum's American Section Gallery, ca. 1912. Neg. G6-10991.

The collection contains objects from approximately two hundred tribes within ten broad geographic regions: Arctic (Plates 1-9); Subarctic (Plates 10-20); Northwest Coast (Plates 21-37); Plateau (Plates 38-41); California (Plates 42-48); Great Basin (Plate 49); Southwest (Plates 50-63); Plains (Plates 64-87); Southeast (Plates 88-94); and Northeast (Plates 95-110) (see Figure 1). While there are many geographical and material strengths of the collection, some portions stand out from the rest due to the fact that they are either unique or rare, large in number, or were acquired according to systematic methods.

Of special note are the Alaskan and Canadian Arctic holdings (Plates 1-9) which represent the north Alaska Coastal Inuit (from the regions of Barrow, Point Hope, and Wainwright), the Inuit from Nunivak Island, the Bering Strait Inuit (in the region between Cape Prince of Wales and Nunivak Island), Mainland Southwest Alaska Inuit in the region of the Kuskokwim River, and central Canada's Copper Inuit and Iglulik peoples.

Particular strengths within the holdings of the Subarctic zone represent Alaska's Holikachuk and Ingalik peoples (Plates 10-11), as well as Labrador's Innu (Naskapi) and Montagnais tribes (Plates 15-18). Of the Museum's large holdings from the Northwest Coast, the Tlingit collection from southeast Alaska acquired by Louis Shotridge is of particular importance (Plates 22-28).

The West and Plains are also well represented. The strongest collections from California represent the northern Pomo and Hupa tribes (Plates 42-48). Collections from the Plateau region represent the Umatilla and Klamath tribes of Oregon. From the Great Basin, the Bannock of Idaho's Fort Hall Reservation, the Shoshone of Wyoming's Wind River Reservation, the Uinta Ute of White Rocks, Utah, and Nevada's Northern Paiute of Pyramid Lake are most numerous (Plates 38-41). Rich collections from the Southwest region (Plates 50-63) include material culture of the Apache, Navajo, and Pueblo peoples. Plains Indian collections represent the Blackfeet, Crow, and Lakota of the Fort Peck Reservation; North Dakota's Devil's Lake Reservation, and South Dakota's Pine Ridge Agency; the Arapaho (both Oklahoma and Wind River Reservation, Wyoming), and the Southern Cheyenne of Oklahoma (Plates 64-87).

The Museum's Eastern holdings include a variety of Iroquois specimens representing each of the six Iroquois nations; a well documented collection of Canadian Algonquin materials from the River Desert Band of Quebec acquired by Frederick Johnson on behalf of Professor Frank G. Speck; and Cherokee material culture from North Carolina acquired by Speck and John Witthoft (Plates 88-110). While it is impossible to describe all of these collections in this Guide, a closer look at some of them will reveal their depth and variety and give a sense of their significance to their makers and collectors.

The Edward Avery McIlhenny Collection

The earliest systematic ethnographic collection of the American Section reflects the close intellectual links between early anthropological collecting and the discipline of natural history. Just as natural scientists used type plant and animal specimens to represent species, early anthropologists used objects to represent whole cultures, replacing original contexts with classificatory schemes. The University Museum quickly outgrew the limiting framework of natural history and turned toward the social sciences, in a move that made it unique among its competitors in Chicago, New York, and Washington. In this vein, Director William Pepper sent a young naturalist named Edward Avery McIlhenny to Alaska in the spring of 1897 with the goals of forming ethnological, archaeological, and natural history collections. As a result 1,600 specimens came to Penn, while the avian and mammalian collections (including 294 bird study skins and more than 300 lemming skulls and furs, with sex, Latin name, and genus noted) were deposited at Philadelphia's Academy of Natural Sciences.

McIlhenny's interest in natural history and especially birds grew out of his Southern upbringing. In 1892, after witnessing the slaughter of thousands of snowy egrets by hunters seeking feathers for ladies' hats, McIlhenny assisted in the negotiations to purchase Louisiana's 200-acre Avery Island to establish a bird sanctuary. The site is maintained today as a state refuge for many species on their seasonal migrations.

In 1896, eager to explore the world's natural habitats, McIlhenny traveled with two assistants to Alaska's most northern feature, Point Barrow, having agreed to gather collections for the Museum. Living in Barrow for a year and a half and through a long and hard winter, he recorded the behavior of fauna within the arctic habitat. In the process, McIlhenny interacted with the local Iñupiaq people, from whom he ultimately acquired 1,589 ethnological specimens for the Museum. He systematically recorded detailed notes including the native linguistic term for each object, the materials used in their construction, and the use or function of each specimen. In addition, McIlhenny took 200 photographs also housed in the Museum. The collection includes an extensive range of fishing and hunting equipment (Plate 3), whaling charms, tools, dance masks, and clothing, many of which incorporate bird and animal parts which were of particular interest to the collector.

Indigenous Arctic peoples maintain strong associations with the birds and animals in their environments, and important ceremonies and rituals are traditionally associated with the feeding of animal spirits to ensure their continued abundance on earth. McIlhenny recorded the function and meaning of several ceremonial objects related to the northern environment. As his collection attests, virtually all traditional Inuit objects are associated in some way with the animal world.

According to the Iñupiaq, animal and human life is controlled by the *tunghat*, spirit keepers believed to live on the moon. Humans demonstrate their respect for them by offering gifts and festivals in their honor and by depicting them in material culture (Plate 1). Similarly, humans can attract and please the animal world by incorporating animal imagery into a multitude of utilitarian and decorative forms. For many Arctic peoples, animals enjoy aspects of personhood and humans are to treat them with respect. Parts of animals are often used as amulets to access the power of their abiding spirits (Plate 6).

Birds, for example, hold a special place in the Inuit and Athapaskan imagination. Often considered messengers from the spirit world, birds move between the sky world and earth playing different roles of communicators of activity. Loons, with their sophisticated abilities to catch fish under water, are often closely associated with the spirit world. Loon calls are known to inspire songs and singing, and their somber calls sometimes bring the bad news that someone will soon die (Plate 10).

Many other birds often provide signs to northern hunters about where animals and fish might be found, and can sometimes even influence animals and fish on a hunter's behalf. Religious leaders often employed bird-helping spirits, donned in the form of a bird mask, for example, to assist them in causing the return of swans, geese, and ducks in the spring to give nourishment to the people. Hunters used bird charms in whaling for speed in travel across the water (Plate 4). Bird elements such as feathers or beaks on masks and clothing are used as a means of honoring the bird spirits (Plate 5). Inuit women are skilled at making beautiful coats of lightweight bird skins and bags out of birds' webbed feet. Hollow bird bones were used to store bird-bone sewing needles, and feathers continue to be used to ornament masks, headdresses, and clothing.

McIlhenny and the northern Inuit shared an interest in the plant and animal species of the Arctic environment, the former as a measure of scientific understanding and conservation and the latter as knowledgeable, believing partners in an ever-changing environment. Today, many northern native villages still retain a strong community identity that is frequently based on the continuance of traditional hunting and fishing. This is often reflected in an ideology that includes a special reverence for elders who retain their cultures' traditional ecological knowledge and spiritual reverence for the land and animals upon whom life depends.

The Stewart Culin Collection

In 1892 Stewart Culin (Figure 3), the son of a Philadelphia merchant, was appointed Curator of General Ethnology at the Museum. He conducted three North American collecting expeditions resulting in 3,000 additions to the ethnological collections. Culin is perhaps best known for his lifelong interest in Native American Indian games.

Culin's first trip was in the company of the highly experienced ethnologist George Dorsey of Chicago's Field Museum. Together they set out in 1900 on a summer tour of Indian reservations between Chicago and San Francisco, north to Victoria, and back east again via the Sioux reserves in Montana and South Dakota. In eleven states, and moving at a fast pace, Culin collected about 1,000 specimens from thirteen tribes including the Sauk and Fox, Arapaho and Shoshone, the Bannock, Uinta Ute, Pyramid Lake Paiute, Hupa, Karok, Makah, Yakima, Umatilla, and several Lakota groups. Culin witnessed the height of the reservation period, with many tribes restricted in their abilities to hunt, and experiencing increased mortality rates and miserable conditions.

Throughout his travels, he gathered information on the rules and materials of games of chance and dexterity and often commissioned game pieces on the spot.

The following summer, Culin traveled briefly to the Hopi Pueblos where he acquired an additional 500 ethnographic baskets, tools, textiles, ceremonial objects, and ceramics for the Museum (Plate 55). Traveling on horseback from village to village, he collected at Hano, Mishongnavi, Oraibi, Shipaulovi, and Walpi.

Internationally known for his museum exhibitions, Culin's collections were enthusiastically reviewed in newspapers and prominently displayed in the Museum's galleries upon his return to Philadelphia. His notes from 1902 reveal a sympathetic tone, mentioning that recent actions by the Bureau of Indian Affairs, such as the abolishment of Indian dances, the strong presence of an externally imposed work ethic, and the extensive influence of Roman Catholicism, were rapidly bringing Pueblo civilization to extinction.

In February of 1902 Culin returned briefly to the Southwest, where he visited New Mexico's Zuni and Isleta Pueblos. On this trip he acquired approximately 200 objects, including toys and games, tools, katsinas, pottery, and ceremonial materials (Plate 53).

In his book *Games of the North American Indians*, Culin demonstrates that games are more than simple entertainment, but rather means of making decisions and predicting the future. He proposed that gaming had its origins in mythology. Native American origin myths, he noted, often describe a series of contests in which a culture hero challenges and overcomes a foe of the human race with trickery, skill, or magic. The principal characters and players are often the twin children of the Sun who live

Figure 3. Stewart Culin, 1900. Neg. S4-140826.

in the east and west, rule night and day, winter and summer, and who embody the morning and evening stars. Always contending, they are the original patrons of play, and their games are the games now played by men. The significant emblems of the twins are their weapons, including wooden throwing clubs, bows and arrows made of cane, and a netted shield. Culin argued that many gaming pieces are linked to these emblems.

Culin's monograph was directly influenced by the work of his colleague, Frank Hamilton Cushing, a Smithsonian anthropologist who had lived among the Zuni from 1879 to 1884. Until Cushing's premature death in 1900, the men shared a strong friendship and mutual interest in games, and examples collected by Cushing (and replicas made by him) are housed in the University Museum. Cushing documented the close association and significance of

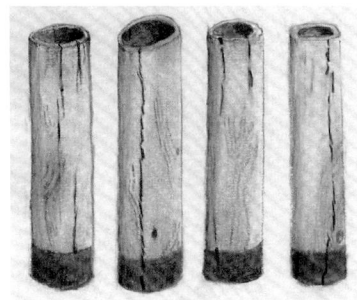

Figure 4. Zuni ball game tubes collected by Stewart Culin, 1902. Drawing by Kevin Lamp.

gaming within the context of the annual ceremonial calendar at Zuni.

According to Cushing several ritualized games are closely associated with the twin war gods, supernatural protectors of the Zuni people who influence weather and prosperity in general and who act as patrons of gaming and sports. The games of the war gods are associated with war and peace, and their play by humans is often a metaphor for renewal and fertility.

The hidden ball game, for example, involves a set of four wooden cylinders with a cavity in one end (Figure 4). Two teams of four men alternate hiding a small round ball within the cylinder. The other team tries to find it through guesswork. Cylinder sets made of cottonwood, the "wood of water" and of life substance, are associated with peace and are played by appropriate clans in spring or early summer just before planting. Game cylinders made of heavy oak are associated with war and are called upon when necessary, usually in the windy season of April and May. Both versions of the game are played to divine answers to questions of war or peace. Oftentimes the questions involve predicting the effects of the wind and water gods upon agriculture. Will it be a dry season or a wet season, and, by the relative scoring of the game, how wet and how dry in regard to the growth of the corn that is about to be planted?

Building on the Zuni example, Culin's monograph presented evidence of more than a thousand game traits gathered from two hundred tribes. He proposed that games played for amusement or personal gain seem to have descended from ceremonial observances and are performed also as religious ceremonies to please the gods to secure their favor, to drive away illness or evil, to produce rain and the fertilization and reproduction of plants and animals, or for other positive results. Culin found similar divinatory rites among indigenous cultures throughout the world.

The George Byron Gordon Collection

When Culin left Penn for the Brooklyn Museum of Art in 1903, George Byron Gordon was hired as Assistant Curator of General Ethnology (Figure 5). An Americanist trained at Harvard University, Gordon had a strong interest in the Museum's educational role and consistently pushed to exhibit as many collections as possible. By 1904 he also held the title of General Curator of American Archaeology. For Gordon, like many scholars of his day, native objects were primary data and needed to be gathered into museums before their producers became extinct. Gordon was highly competitive and throughout his twenty-four-year career with the Museum urged his field agents to acquire old (thus traditional), "museum-quality" collections. Such collections would enable the Museum to produce exhibitions that would outdo those of his rivals at the American Museum in New York and elsewhere.

In 1905 Gordon planned his first ethnological collecting expedition to Alaska with the goals of rounding out the McIlhenny collection and salvaging ethnographic information in "untouched" areas. Spending the summer season among Inuit peoples on the coast of the Bering Sea (an area that was not untouched), Gordon visited eighteen communities, collecting over

Figure 5. George B. Gordon in Alaska, 1905. Neg. S4-143057.

1,500 specimens and taking 300 photographs (Figure 6). These collections from Nunivak Island, Cape Prince of Wales, St. Michael, King Island, Diomede Island, Cape Nome, Unalakleet, Kotzebue Sound, Kuskokwim Bay, and East Cape Siberia include large quantities of hide clothing, boots, mittens, and bags, as well as ceremonial items, tools, paddles, and kayaks (Plate 4). Trained as an archaeologist, Gordon knew the importance of documentation, and though his notations are not especially detailed, provenience and source information are always present on acquisitions made directly from the natives. On his way home Gordon also purchased Tlingit collections from the village of Klukwan. Continually in pursuit of objects of the highest quality, Gordon established a network of local collectors who would continue to act as field agents and suppliers throughout his career.

Gordon returned to Alaska in 1907, financed in part by his friend, the New

Figure 6. Native berry pickers from Cape Prince of Wales at Nome, Alaska, ca. 1905. Photographer unidentified. Neg. S8-138917.

York businessman and inveterate collector George G. Heye. This time Gordon went to the interior where he traveled by canoe on the Kuskokwim River. He acquired 300 items such as tools for hunting and fishing, wooden buckets, snowshoes, lamps, baskets, clothing, and earrings for the Museum, and traded duplicates to Heye (Plate 5). That same year Gordon arranged to house and exhibit Heye's large and broad collection of American Indian materials at the Museum, with the expectation that some day it would become part of the Museum's permanent collection. For the next nine years Heye would remain closely associated with the Museum where he served on the Board of Overseers and financed North American collecting expeditions.

Gordon became director of UPM in 1910. He was instrumental in establishing the University's Anthropology Department and worked for the next seventeen years to increase the Museum's rate of acquisition from cultures around the globe. Because of his already established interest in Alaska, and the presence of the extensive Heye collection, Gordon systematically developed the Museum's Arctic holdings from both Alaska and Canada.

Major acquisitions include an Iglulik Eskimo collection from central Canada acquired in 1911 by Captain George Comer, an accomplished whaler from Connecticut. Comer completed six whaling and trading voyages to Hudson Bay between 1875 and 1919. Though his main purpose was to secure whale oil, baleen, and skins, he became an active collector of scientific information and material culture from the region (Plate 8). In 1914 Gordon purchased a smaller collection of carvings from the same region (Chesterfield Inlet), acquired by Henry Ford, and a Copper Eskimo collection of 275 specimens from northern central Canada's Coppermine River and Coronation Gulf region collected by Captain Joseph Bernard. Gordon went on to purchase Bering Sea and Bering Strait Eskimo and Athapaskan collections acquired by William B. Van Valin in 1918 and 130 Tlingit objects acquired from Navy Lieutenant George T. Emmons in 1918 (Plate 31). Positioned in Alaska in 1882 where law enforcement and peacekeeping duties placed him in frequent contact with the Tlingit, Emmons was a major and reliable source of native-made objects for virtually all of the competing museums.

In addition to developing the Alaskan and Canadian Arctic holdings, when possible, Gordon acquired collections from other regions of North America, though with less intensity due to the presence of Heye's collection (Plates 12, 14, 74). Quality collections came from a variety of sources. In 1907, for example, Gordon acquired the F. S. Plimpton collection of California basketry. In 1910 he briefly hired Gerda Sebbelov, a student of Franz Boas, to complete a study on Osage women's art in Oklahoma, a project that was largely unsuccessful but resulted in a small Osage collection. From Frank Gist, a trader at Hupa, California, Gordon acquired a variety of items in 1912. In 1916 he purchased a trunk of Plains Indian materials, largely of Lakota origin, from Mrs. Mary A. Thompson of Fairfax, South Dakota (Plates 69, 80, 100). In 1918 he purchased the large and well-documented Deisher collection of California basketry compiled from many tribes primarily before 1907 (Plate 43).

In 1916, much to Gordon's surprise and great disappointment, Heye withdrew his collection from the Museum to create his own New York institution, the Museum of the American Indian, Heye Foundation. This collection is exhibited today at the Gustav Heye Center in New York City and is the centerpiece of the Smithsonian's National Museum of the American Indian.

As a token of his appreciation to the University Museum for housing his collection, Heye offered a gift of 1,200 American Indian objects. The majority of the specimens come from southwestern Canada and include items of Kwakw<u>a</u>ka'wakw (Kwakiutl), Haida, Nuu-cha-nulth (Nootka), Bella Bella, and Tlingit origin (Plate 30). Approximately 150 specimens from the eastern Plains are of Lakota and Osage manufacture. The collection consists primarily of tools, baskets, knives, spoons, bowls, and fish hooks. In addition, many of the items are tourist art. Often criticized for his lack of attention to documentation, Heye was more interested in the objects themselves. He did, however, hire skilled anthropologists to collect for him. These individuals included Frank G. Speck among the Delaware, W. C. Orchard among the Sioux, and M. R. Harrington who collected from many different groups in Oklahoma and the Southwest. In most cases Heye's assistants recorded a wealth of information on the sources and functions of each object.

The Louis Shotridge Collection

Perhaps the most exceptional of the Museum's ethnographic collections is that amassed by Louis Shotridge, a native Tlingit Indian born of a noble family from the southeastern Alaskan village of Klukwan (Figure 7). Shotridge was the first Northwest Coast native person employed full-time by a museum and served as Assistant Curator from 1915 to 1932.

Shotridge was comfortable interacting with the English-speaking world, as his father and grandfather had had a long history of associations with Euro-Americans, and he had been educated in a Presbyterian mission school. He was also familiar with the curio and collecting trades, which were by this time well established in the Northwest Coast. In developing and sustaining his twenty-five-year relationship with the Museum, Shotridge participated in Philadelphia's academic circles as a museum-trained native ethnographer. He simultaneously pursued two goals, to record the history of his own Tlingit culture through its clan art and to exhibit his culture on the stage of a major world museum. At this time, many

Figure 7. "After the first snow, and no snowshoes." Photo by Louis Shotridge, ca. 1918. Neg. 14848.

Tlingit communities were in the process of assimilating to Western society, patrilineal inheritance, and Christianity, and the traditional objects that Shotridge collected were seen by some Tlingit at the time as old fashioned, negative, and the subject of continued rivalry.

George Gordon, then Curator of the Museum's American Section, met Shotridge and his wife, Florence, in 1905 at the Lewis and Clark Centennial Exposition in Portland, Oregon, where Florence was demonstrating traditional Chilkat weaving and Louis had brought Tlingit artifacts to sell. Gordon, en route home from his first Alaskan collecting expedition, recognized the potential of the Tlingit native in acquiring collections for the Museum. In time, with Gordon's support and funded by another Museum benefactor, John Wanamaker, Shotridge would conduct two formal collecting expeditions, resulting in the acquisition of 300 objects.

Gordon was adamant that Shotridge acquire old objects of the highest quality and that they be accompanied by contextual information that would allow the Philadelphia audience to understand their use. Gordon trained Shotridge in scientific documentation and in 1914 sent him briefly to New York City to study linguistics with Franz Boas. Together, over a two-month period, Boas and Shotridge developed the first accurate Tlingit phonology, later used by Shotridge in his documentation and published by Boas and the Museum in 1917. Shotridge may have been the first indigenous transcriber and translator of Tlingit oral literature, and possibly the first Northwest Coast native with professional training in linguistics and anthropology.

Shotridge was not always successful in his collecting activities, and on at least a few occasions controversy emerged over the sale of objects. Responding to offers from headmen, chiefs, and house leaders, and, on some occasions from leading women, Shotridge carefully selected historically significant specimens, sometimes negotiating the purchase price over a one- or two-year period. In this way, he acquired Tlingit clan hats, headdresses, masks, clothing, baskets, rattles, batons, spoons and dishes, and a small number of tools including fishing and hunting equipment, knives, and raw materials (Plates 22-28). In Philadelphia, the items were incorporated into exhibitions where they would represent the history of the Tlingit people for generations to come.

Shotridge's overall strategy was to collect examples of clan art that best represented Tlingit social history and political structure and to show the greatness of Tlingit art. The value of these objects was changing within many Tlingit communities because of the ongoing conversion to

Figure 8. "Two Tlingit girls." Photo by Louis Shotridge, ca. 1920. Neg. S4-14868.

Protestant Christianity and increasing conflict between native matrilineal and Euro-American patrilineal systems of inheritance. In documenting clan identities through Tlingit art, Shotridge foresaw the waning of the clan system as a political unit.

Shotridge developed a systematic method and style of documentation. Traveling regularly to remote villages by boat, he recorded the history of each object as well as genealogical notes in a card file. In the spring of 1917, for example, he acquired three hats from the leader of Klukwan's Kaagwaantaan clan Drum House and recorded their histories (Plate 23). The Undersea Grizzly Bear hat (left) was made for Daqu-tonk of the Kaagwaantaan clan of Chilkat, the first successful leader of his house group. When Daqu-tonk died, he was succeeded by his nephew Gahi and the Killer Whale hat (right) was made for him. The rights to the Killer Whale crest had been won in war with the Naanyaa.aayí clan, and came to be used as an emblem of courage. After Gahi died, his brother Yikashaw inherited the office and as head of the House commissioned the "Murrelet" hat (center) to represent the Neix.ádi clan.

At Gordon's urging, Shotridge also paid special attention to legends and myths and, when possible, made sound recordings; he also took a total of 500 photographic images of his local surroundings, individuals, and objects (Figure 8). In addition, Shotridge wrote fourteen detailed essays situating Tlingit objects within their socio-historic clan contexts, which were published in the *Museum Journal*.

Shotridge valued both traditional and modern Tlingit lifeways. Through his object collections, photographs, and writings, he established an authentic record of Tlingit society as it was changing by illustrating Tlingit objects within their particular socio-historical, house group, and clan contexts. Shotridge participated in traditional ceremonial activities, and like many in his community, openly regretted their decline. He was also involved in the Alaska Native Brotherhood (ANB), a powerful indigenous organization founded in 1912 to promote the social and civil welfare of the Indians of Alaska. Shotridge was elected president of the ANB in 1930. The ANB succeeded in convincing the Alaska legislature to pass the first antidiscrimination law in the nation in 1946, twenty years before the national Civil Rights movement. As his collections, writings, and photographs reveal, Shotridge worked to preserve Tlingit heritage and to achieve civil equality for Native Alaskans.

Many of the objects Shotridge acquired have been prominently exhibited at the Museum in displays about Tlingit culture and heritage since their arrival in Philadelphia in the 1920s. As Shotridge wished, in this setting the accomplishments of Tlingit culture and art can be viewed among the great cultures of Egypt, Asia, Mesopotamia, and the Maya world.

The Frank G. Speck Collection

Frank G. Speck (Figure 9) was an ethnologist and a major force in establishing Penn's Department of Anthropology. He conducted research on the native peoples of the eastern region of North America, resulting in over fifty studies related to at least thirty different native groups. He acquired approximately 800 Innu (Naskapi), Cherokee, Iroquois, and Canadian Algonquian specimens for the Museum. His collections reveal his strong and continued interest in religion and art, as well as his fundamental belief that objects, like myths, rituals, tales, and songs, are manifestations of Native American world views. Speck's collections are meticulously documented. The unique strengths of the documentation can be seen in the detailed recording of the social contexts of each object and in the notations of the underlying processes surrounding each object's origin, manufacture, and use.

Figure 9. Frank G. Speck (rear) with Cayuga informants, ca. 1940. Neg. S4-143974.

Though Speck himself was not Mohegan, he was raised in rural Connecticut by a Mohegan Indian woman, Mrs. Fidelia Fielding, one of a few remaining speakers of the Pequot language. In her household, Speck became fluent in Pequot at an early age and developed a deep appreciation of native values and culture. Trained by Boas in comparative linguistics at Columbia University, Speck completed his dissertation on the ethnography of the Oklahoma Yuchi. He came to the Museum on a fellowship in 1907 and became assistant professor of anthropology in 1911.

Speck pursued fieldwork among the small hunting bands living north of the Gulf of the St. Lawrence, where Innu Eskimos hunted in winter in Labrador and the Laurentian Islands, and gathered in summer fishing camps on the north shore. In 1929, 1930, and 1931 Speck made significant collections from the region, and his work resulted in his perhaps best-known ethnography, *Naskapi: Savage Hunters of the Labrador Peninsula* (1935). From 1932 to 1940 Speck also worked with one of his students, John Witthoft, among North Carolina's Big Cove Band of the Eastern Cherokee. Their joint research resulted in a collection of 300 specimens (Plates 90 and 94). Speck also conducted many years of research and collaboration among the Iroquois, and well-documented collections from those groups have come to the Museum via another Speck student, Samuel Fernberger (Plate 107).

A brief look at Speck's Innu study highlights the larger context and significance of that collection and the meaning of material culture for the Innu people themselves (Plates 15-18). Speck's goal was to understand the underlying belief system connecting objects and ways of life to the supernatural world. He identified the concept of reciprocity as central to the dynamic relationship between humans and nature.

The Innu are Algonquian-speaking people who, in the early 1930s, were living in isolation and at the barest subsistence level in eastern Canada (Figure 10). For the Innu, the hunting of caribou, bear, deer, and beaver is a sacred occupation. The Innu believe that the difference between humans and animals lies only in outward form, and thus in a spiritual sense, they are considered equal. The killing of animals therefore requires knowledge of traditional rules of conduct which are to be carried out by each hunter. Success in hunting and in life depends on this knowledge. Lack of skill in the tracking of animals, or in the disappearance of game from the hunter's territory, would result in famine, starvation, sickness, and death. All are attributed to either the hunter's ignorance of a hidden principle of behavior toward the animals or to his willful disregard of them.

For the Innu, an individual's soul or "great man" spirit is that which guides one through life and which provides the means for overcoming the spirits of animals in the lifelong search of animals for food. The Innu state:

> The "great man" reveals itself in dreams. Every individual has one and every individual has dreams. Those who respond to their dreams by giving them serious attention, by thinking about them, by trying to interpret their meaning in secret and testing out their truth, can cultivate deeper communication with the "great man." He then favors such a person with more dreams, and these better in quality. The next obligation is for the individual to follow instruction given him in dreams, and to memorialize them in representations of art. (Speck 1935: 35)

Dreams tell hunters where to go for game and how to satisfy the animal's spirit when it is killed. By ignoring one's dreams, an individual would loose his or her powerful and far-seeing spirit guide and would be doomed to failure and starvation. As a "great man" becomes more active, he requires that the individual tell no lies and behave generously to others and to the animal world.

How is this concept of the soul spirit expressed in Innu material culture? Speck shows that the Innu "great man" spirit requires that objects, creatures, colors, and materials presented to men and women in dreams must be represented graphically or by symbols so their power can be used to bring success to that individual in his or her activities. As a result, designs on hide clothing (Plate 15), in beadwork (Plate 16), or on birchbark represent trees, plants, animals, occasionally humans, and often celestial phenomena. This process involves an analogy between the forms that are depicted and the control/power over the animal in bringing the thing depicted under human control. The spirit is satisfied by seeing its suggestions followed and displayed in artwork. Thus, caribou skin boots, hats, mittens, bags, and coats are decorated in particular ways to help subdue the game. In short, the animals prefer to be killed by hunters whose clothing is decorated with designs, and the souls of the hunters like to see them dressed and decorated in colors. Dreams of animals are understood as wishes that the man will give that animal a gift, a responsibility that the hunter accepts by decorating an article of apparel or use in a particular way.

In understanding the Innu perspective, it is clear that the reciprocal act of creating material culture is at the heart of maintaining an essential balance for life. Through his detailed accounts, Speck's work reveals an underlying indigenous framework that relates Innu material culture to its larger context.

NAGPRA and Beyond

A new phase in the relationship of museums and native peoples was marked by the passage of the Native American Graves Protection and Repatriation Act (NAGPRA) in 1990. The Museum and the American Section have been actively involved in an ongoing dialogue with Native American and Native Hawaiian groups to reevaluate the ownership of human remains, funerary and sacred objects, and objects of cultural patrimony in the Museum's collections. The repatriation movement represents an effort on the part of Native Americans to reconstitute a collective cultural identity in the aftermath of colonialism. The related legislation, which mandates that museums repatriate, to federally recognized entities, human remains and objects meeting particular definitions, provides one framework for communication between museums and Native Americans.

NAGPRA has created an improved understanding and awareness on the Museum's part of a host of contemporary issues important to native peoples. Some of the issues surround the respectful handling and treatment of human remains and sacred objects, and others involve the ongoing significance of objects to native communities. As of this writing, the Museum has received 35 claims for a total of 237 human remains and 1,405 objects of cultural patrimony and

Figure 10. "Young Gerome," one of Speck's informants. Montagnais-Naskapi, St. Augustine Band. Photo by Frank G. Speck, 1935. Neg. S4-143941.

sacred objects. Of these, 19 claims have been approved by the Museum Committee on Repatriation and the Board of Trustees of the University of Pennsylvania, one claim has been denied, three claims have been withdrawn by native entities, and twelve claims are in process.

NAGPRA consultations have involved considerable discussion, research, and learning for both parties, and this has resulted in significant new relationships with many groups. An example is the Museum's long-term loan of a wooden mask to the Mohegan of Connecticut (Plate 108), an association that acknowledges our historical relationship with the tribe through Gladys Tantaquidgeon and Frank G. Speck and our support of the tribe's educational goals. NAGPRA has also challenged the Museum to grow in new ways and to understand ownership from the native point of view. In the process, many native groups have expressed their gratitude for the Museum's role in preserving their objects. As a result of sharing of information, many improvements have been made to the Museum's records, and contemporary objects have been added to the collections (Plates 7 and 10).

The Museum is committed to understanding and documenting native ways of life and values in the 21st century. Although funds for collecting activities are limited, recent acquisitions have been made from the Alaskan Arctic (Plate 10), the Northwest Coast (Plate 36), the Pueblo Southwest (Plates 58–61, 63), and the Southeast (Plate 93).

Several related questions inform the American Section's collecting strategy. How are contemporary native artists interpreting their rich cultural heritage, and how does this relate to or have an impact on their traditional arts? What goals do individual artists have, and how might these reflect or differ from those of their communities? How do artists draw from old ideas to create something new and individual? What roles do these new objects play within their own communities today?

The Museum is working assiduously to expand the use of its collections and to make them available to native communities. Examples include loans (Plate 108) and traveling exhibitions, our ongoing collaboration with the National Museum of the American Indian's artist-in-residence program (Plates 33, 35, 57, 81, 93), the production of publications, sharing of images and information, and encouragement offered to native people to participate in Museum activities (Plate 46).

In the early 1990s UPM worked with a team of native advisors to develop the exhibition "Living in Balance: The Universe of the Hopi, Zuni, Navajo, and Apache." The primary goal of the exhibit and accompanying catalogue was to use the Museum's 100-year-old collections to explain the essential ideas that continue to define and shape each of these group's world views.

More recently, Raymond Dutchman's contemporary masks were inspired by 100-year-old masks in the collection that reminded him of events and masking traditions no longer practiced in his own Alaskan community (Plate 10).

Arwen Nuttall, tribal member of the Four Winds Band of the Louisiana Cherokee Confederacy and Museum Intern, used Stewart Culin's collection to develop an educational program on Native American games (Plate 56). Using games from a variety of tribes, she explains their uses in recreation and ceremony, to resolve conflict, and to train individuals in skills needed for future success. By using games to teach visitors about native skills and ways of learning, Nuttall's overarching goal is to dispel stereotypes of Native Americans.

Jerry Ingram, a Choctaw artist, studied the Museum's collection to gain insight into the style and construction techniques of Southeastern shoulder bags. The information gathered has influenced his work (Plate 93).

Many native people have a strong adherence to and respect for tradition, innovation, and craftsmanship, and museums which house old collections are uniquely positioned to offer keys to understanding those traditions in support of modern goals. This issue will remain at the forefront of our work in the years to come.

Ethnographic objects participate in different spheres of knowledge and power. In the process of collecting, the voices and stories of an object's origins and meaning are sometimes silenced in favor of new ones about progress and civilization. For McIlhenny, Culin, and Gordon, ethnographic objects were seen as representations of pre-modern authentic American Indians and were often presented as traits, anonymously and without histories. In 1916, for example, Gordon was not particularly interested in the fact that the Lakota warrior American Horse had owned a specific war shirt (Plate 69), but was more concerned that such a shirt authentically represent Plains culture in general.

For Shotridge and Speck, objects embodied distinctive histories. Their deep interest in understanding and documenting the specific circumstances surrounding the origins and uses of the objects they collected is seen in their recording of detailed native accounts. In these two cases, the collector's insights enable us to understand something of the central role that objects play in maintaining the social order. For the Naskapi, the reciprocal act of creating gifts of beauty is essential for life. And for the Tlingit, important clan objects often serve as actual embodiments of myth, history, and social status.

The University of Pennsylvania Museum's Native American collections contain outstanding examples of indigenous technologies which reflect ways of life that date largely to the 19th and early 20th centuries. These collections inspire and hold meaning for Native Americans and non-native peoples at many different levels and remind us all that human beings are uniquely dependent on material culture to support and enrich our lives. They also reveal the ingenuity and skill of Native peoples in addressing social and ecological issues, and they document the holistic and reciprocal relationships that Native Americans actively maintain with their universe. Because of the political and social challenges that endure for Native Americans today, museums housing American Indian materials have a special obligation to facilitate collaborations across Native and non-native communities and to encourage ongoing interpretation of these collections.

Readings

Berman, Judith. "Building a Collection: Native Californian Basketry at the University of Pennsylvania Museum." *Expedition* 40, no. 1(1998): 23-33.

Blankenship, Roy, ed. *The Life and Times of Frank G. Speck, 1881-1950*. University of Pennsylvania Publications in Anthropology no. 4. Philadelphia: University of Pennsylvania Department of Anthropology, 1991.

Culin, Stewart. *Games of the North American Indians*. Smithsonian Institution, Bureau of American Ethnology, Annual Report 24. Washington, DC: U.S. Government Printing Office, 1907. Reprint, New York: Dover, 1975.

Dauenhauer, Nora. "Tlingit At.oow: Traditions and Concepts." In *The Spirit Within: Northwest Coast Native Art from the John H. Hauberg Collection*. Seattle: Seattle Art Museum, 1995.

Kaplan, Susan A., and Kristin J. Barsness. *Raven's Journey: The World of Alaska's Native People*. Philadelphia: The University Museum, University of Pennsylvania, 1986.

Hinsley, Curtis M. *The Smithsonian and the American Indian: Making a Moral Anthropology in Victorian America*. Washington, DC: Smithsonian Institution Press, 1981.

Milburn, Maureen. "The Politics of Possession: Louis Shotridge and the Tlingit Collection of the University of Pennsylvania Museum." Ph.D. dissertation, University of British Columbia, 1997.

Speck, Frank G. *Naskapi: The Savage Hunters of the Labrador Peninsula*. Norman, OK: University of Oklahoma Press, 1935.

Sturtevant, William C., series ed. *Handbook of North American Indians*. Washington, DC: Smithsonian Institution, 1978- .

Washburn, Dorothy K. *Living in Balance: The Universe of the Hopi, Zuni, Navajo and Apache*. Philadelphia: University of Pennsylvania Museum of Archaeology and Anthropology, 1995.

Wheat, Joe Ben. *The Gift of Spider Woman. Southwestern Textiles: The Navajo Tradition*. Philadelphia: The University Museum, University of Pennsylvania, 1984.

Plates

Plate 1. Yup'ik shaman used masks to influence animal spirits to assist humans in procuring food. The face of the mask represents the moon where the animal spirits dwell, and the holes represent passages between sky and land through which the animals must pass to replenish earth. Yup'ik, Alaska, collected by J. M. Wilcox, 1901. W. 71 cm. NA11783.

Plate 2. Wooden visors were worn by hunters as they hunted seals from their kayaks. The carved ivory elements may refer to the hunter's helping spirits. Yup'ik or Iñupiaq, Norton Sound, Alaska, collected by whaling Captain Joseph Bernard in 1915. H. 36 cm. NA4252.

Plate 3. Bolas were thrown by Iñupiaq duck hunters at oncoming flocks. In flight, the end weights of ivory and walrus bone spread out the sinew strings, catching around a bird's wings and body and bringing it to earth. Iñupiaq, Point Barrow, Alaska, collected by E. A. McIlhenny, 1897. 41480 (top), L. 25 cm extended; 41470 (bottom), L. 51 cm extended.

Plate 4. Bird charms were given as gifts to bird spirits to ensure their abundance and protection on earth. Yup'ik, King Island, Alaska, collected by George Gordon in 1905. L. 28 cm. NA319.

Plate 5. Ceremonial gloves made of seal skin and decorated with puffin beaks and feathers suggest the healing power of the human hand, a prominent theme in Yup'ik oral literature and art. Kusquqvagmiut, Kuskokwim River, Alaska, collected by George Gordon in 1907. H. 45 cm. NA1551.

Plate 6. Fish spirits are imbued with both protective and dangerous qualities. In some regions, families dressed their children in fishskin garments as a safeguard from harmful spirits. Yu'pik girl's parka, Alaska, purchased by George Gordon from E. E. Patterson in 1915. L. 74.5 cm. NA3225.

Plate 7. Cotton *atigluk* such as these modern examples are worn at whaling celebrations today by North Slope Iñupiaq men (left) and women (right). North Slope Iñupiaq, Point Barrow, Alaska, 1997, donated by Michael K. Pederson. 97-25-2, L. 98.5 cm; 97-25-3, L. 122 cm.

Plate 8. This Iglulik woman's inner parka (*atigi*) from central Canada is made of caribou skin. The hood is sized to accommodate a baby, supported by straps on the wearer's back. The beadwork patterns parallel traditional tattoo designs. A topsail schooner, possibly the collector's ship the *Era*, is depicted at the base of the hood, upside down in this plate. Iglulik, Repulse Bay region, Canada, ca. 1910, collected by whaling Captain George Comer. Front length 82 cm. NA2844.

Plate 9. This Loucheux Athapaskan (northern Alaska) summer outfit, ca. 1850, includes a tunic, pants with moccasins attached, and mittens made from tanned caribou or moose hide. It is decorated with porcupine quills, glass beads, dentalium shell, feathers, and arm bands. Loucheux, Alaska, purchased by George Gordon in 1908. NA7739a (tunic) L. 114 cm; NA7739b (pants), L. 88 cm; and NA7740 (mittens), L. 24 cm.

Plate 10 (*above*). Old masks in the Museum's collection (right) inspired Alaskan Ingalik wood carver Raymond Dutchman to make these modern examples of Wildman (left) and loon (right). Masks are no longer used in dances at his Athapaskan village of Shageluk, where modern carvings such as these decorate native homes today. Museum purchase. 2001-19-2, H. 50 cm; 2001-19-1, H. 46 cm.

Plate 11. These dance masks depict Wildman, a part human, part animal creature who inhabits Alaska's Koyukon and Holikachuk wilderness. Wildman's mythological origins tell that anyone driven to the point of surviving on human flesh will vanish into the forest, lose fundamental qualities of humanity, and never return to society. Ingalik, Anvik, Alaska, purchased in 1917 from Leo Demoski. NA5831c, H. 43 cm; NA5831b, H. 42 cm.

Plate 12. This elkskin coat exemplifies the northern Athapaskan women's tradition of decorative hand-loom weaving with porcupine quills. A small number of women at Fort Providence, west of the Northwest Territory's Great Slave Lake, continue to weave distinctive quill bands today. Loucheaux or Slavey, late 19th century, collected by George Gordon in 1915. L. 83 cm. NA3635.

Plate 13. These caribou skin mittens were made around 1950 by Mrs. John, an Ahtna woman from the Athapaskan village of Mentasta located on Alaska's Upper Copper River. Donated by Frederica de Laguna. L. 32.5 cm. 93-1-1.

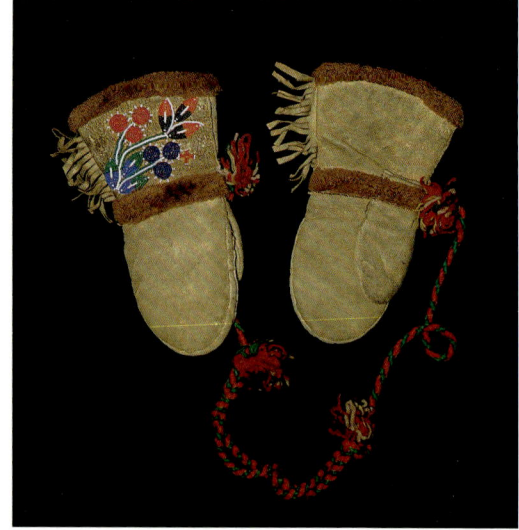

Plate 14. Chilcotin baskets from the southern Subarctic region of the Thompson and Fraser rivers in the interior of British Columbia are coiled of cedar root and decorated with strips of folded beargrass. Rigid and well suited for food gathering and storage, these baskets were also used for cooking with heated rocks. Purchased by George Gordon from J. H. Allice, 1915.

Plate 15. Critical to their survival, the Innu (Naskapi) enlisted the aid of the caribou by making and wearing painted coats to ensure a successful hunt. The coats lost their power by the end of each hunting season and new ones were made annually. Man's summer hunting coat, Innu, Labrador, Barren Ground Band, collected by Frank Speck in 1931. L. 106 cm. 31-7-5.

Plate 16. Shot bags carried by Innu (Naskapi) hunters were worn on the chest with the strap around the neck. The central design motif represents the hunter's 'great man' spirit. The bags act as talismans through which the owner's spirits gain control over those of the game animals. Innu, Labrador, Barren Ground Band, collected by Frank Speck in 1930–31. 31-7-24, L. 19 cm; 30-3-31, L. 20 cm; 31-7-25, L. 22 cm.

Plate 17. Animal drag strings used to bring otters home from the hunt were essential tools for Innu (Naskapi) hunters in the 1930s. The respect and ritual with which animals are treated is central to the success of Innu men and women throughout their lives. Innu, Labrador, Barren Ground Band, collected by Frank Speck, 1930. L. 600 cm. 30-3-208.

Plate 18. In the 1930s the Innu (Naskapi) of Labrador practiced divination to seek guidance and direction on issues such as sickness, famine, failure, and success. One form of divination, still used by some Innu today, involves holding an animal bone over a flame and interpreting the resulting spots, cracks, and breaks. Collected by Frank Speck in 1931. 70-9-513, fetal caribou leg bones (top left), L. 4.5 cm; 70-9-514 bear knee bone (bottom left), L. 4 cm; 31-7-171a,b rabbit scapulae, L. 5.5 cm (top) and 6.5 cm.

Plate 19. Beadwork remains a woman's art today in the Subarctic where skills are passed down from mother to daughter or through more formal instruction in classes or community centers. Man's moosehide coat, Cree, Cold Lake Band, purchased by Frank G. Speck in 1931. L. 67 cm. 31-7-185.

Plate 20. Padded horse saddles were made and used by Algonquian-speaking Cree peoples south of Hudson Bay. Floral beadwork patterns became popular in the 19th century. Cree, collected by I. C. Woodruff, U.S. Brigadier General between 1849 and 1852. W. (from front to back) 43 cm. 81-28-1.

Plate 21. This Tlingit artist's pattern set contains 70 cedar bark patterns of various sizes, many of which are painted. The curved oval shape is a fundamental design element of the Tlingit artistic tradition used in wood carving, painting, weaving, and metalwork. The container is made from the stomach of a sea lion. Klukwan, Alaska, collected by George Gordon in 1905. Gutskin container, NA1279, L. 78 cm.

Plate 22 (*opposite, top*). These clan hats represent the history and strengths of the Kaagwaantaan Clan, the most powerful of the Tlingit Wolf moiety. Louis Shotridge collected them between 1924 and 1926 and noted that the Eagle hat (center front) symbolizes the clan's determination; the Killer Whale hat (center back) represents the maritime power of the clan; the Killer Whale woven hat (left) was that of the first woman diplomat; and the Ganook Hat (right) represents the most ancient being in Tlingit mythology who controls nature. Tlingit, Alaska. NA11742, H. 25 cm; NA11741, H. 27 cm; NA11743; NA6864, H. 38 cm.

Plate 23 (*opposite*). Louis Shotridge acquired these hats from Daqu-tonk, the leader of the Kaagwaantaan Clan's Drum House at the Alaskan village of Klukwan in the spring of 1917. Undersea Grizzly Bear helmet (left), NA5739, H. 35 cm; Killer Whale hat (right), NA5738, H. 42 cm; Murrelet hat (center), NA5740, H. 25 cm.

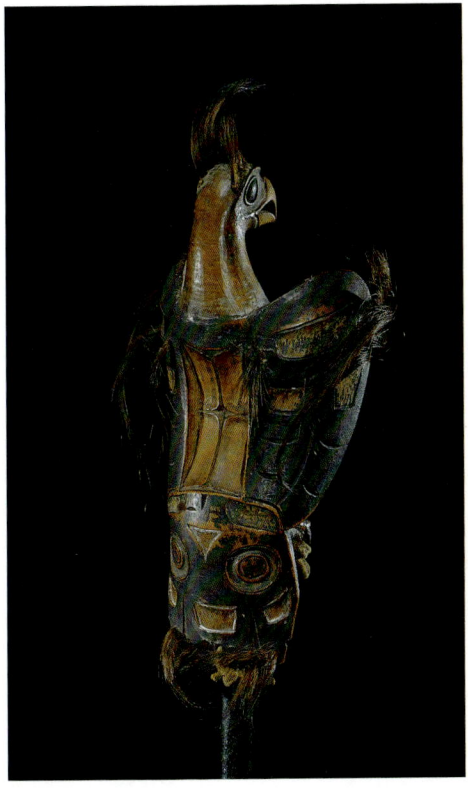

Plate 24. Tlingit scholar and collector Louis Shotridge noted that clan rights to the eagle as an emblem of determination belonged to the Wolf moiety. This staff head was the original object the people carried when they took possession of the region, and its image was later used as a crest on a ceremonial headdress. Tlingit, Alaska, collected by Louis Shotridge in 1923. H. 18 cm. NA9468.

Plate 25 (*above and opposite*). Shotridge acquired these decorative interior house posts depicting a bear in 1930 from his own family's Fin House at the northern Tlingit village of Klukwan. H. 230 cm. 31-29-13,14,15,16.

Plate 26. This Tlingit man's tunic depicting a grizzly bear was acquired by Louis Shotridge in 1926 at the village of Killisnoo on Alaska's Admiralty Island. Shotridge noted that it depicts the main crest of the once-great clan of the Hootsnuwoo, Teikweidí, Raven House. L. 132 cm. NA 10829.

Plate 27. This beaded shirt of red woolen trade cloth depicts a spotted frog emerging from his house. Several Tlingit lineages, such as the Kiks.ádi, claim the frog as a crest. Tlingit, Alaska, collected by Louis Shotridge in 1923. L. 93 cm. NA9483.

Plate 28a. This Tlingit wooden staff depicts an octopus tentacle. Shotridge noted that it was known to be [one of] the best pieces of the Lukna-adi Clan, and one of the most famous objects of the Tlingit people. Collected by Louis Shotridge from the Sitka Whale Collection in 1925. L. 157 cm. NA10513.

Plate 28b (*left*). Detail of NA10513.

Plate 29 (*below*). This wooden food bowl was donated to the UPM by the renowned anthropologist, Frederica de Laguna. Associated with the Museum for over 70 years, de Laguna conducted important archaeological and ethnographic research in Alaska. Her work on the Tlingit of Yakutat, *Under Mount Saint Elias* (1972), is the most complete description of any American Indian tribe. Tlingit, Alaska, collected by Eleanor Bliss in 1893. H. 19.5 cm. 99-19-1.

Plate 30. In 1918 George G. Heye gave 1,200 items to the Museum, the majority of which represent Northwest Coast Indian tourist art. 29-175-345, box (top left), Haida, H. 31.5 cm; 29-175-69 model totem, Haida, H. 43 cm; 29-48-319 mask (top right), Kwakwaka'wakw, H. 34 cm; 29-175-278 sea lion dish (bottom left), Kwakwaka'wakw, L. 40 cm; 29-175-284 seal dish (bottom right), Haida, L. 23.5 cm.

Plate 31. "Coppers" were owned by Northwest Coast chiefs and leading families and represented a concentration of wealth. Originally made of native copper, they were sometimes given individual names and were used as symbolic displays of status. Undersea grizzly bear, Tlingit, Alaska, ca. 1910, collected by Navy Lieutenant George T. Emmons. H. 39 cm. 29-31-1.

Plate 32. For many native North American peoples, masks play a vital role in the enactment and preservation of native stories, myths, and values. This Haida wooden mask represents the face of a mythic noblewoman whose high status is signified by her lip ornament and red face paint. The reverse side is rigged with a piece of rawhide which was held between the wearer's teeth to hold the mask in place when worn in performance. British Columbia, collected originally by William Clark 1804–1806. Charles H. Stephens Collection. H. 23 cm. 45-15-2.

Plate 33. Silas Art Saunders is a self-taught Nuxalt (Bella Coola) wood carver from the coastal community of Bella Coola, British Columbia. Shown here researching Nuxalt collections at the UPM in 1999, Silas's goal is to preserve the old ways by sharing them with younger generations.

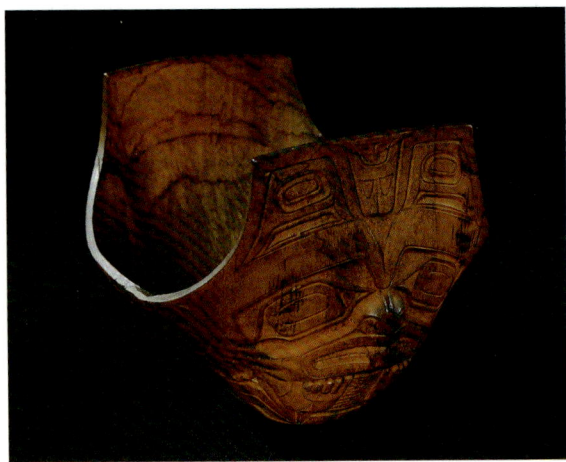

Plate 34. This graceful bowl made from mountain sheep horn exemplifies the highly developed skill in carving and design that many Northwest Coast artists possess. The bowl depicts a beaver, with straight teeth and cross-hatched tail. It was collected in 1885 by Lydia Morris, whose family founded a school of horticulture and botany that survives today as Penn's Morris Arboretum. Haida, British Columbia. H. 14 cm. NA 4291.

Plate 35. Evelyn Vanderhoop (Haida) is one of a small number of Northwest Coast artists with the knowledge and skill to produce traditional hand-woven Raven's Tail and Chilkat-style weavings. Vanderhoop visited the Museum in 2000 to examine specific techniques used to join selvedge braids to the main body of robes, artists' signatures which are incorporated into each weaving, and robe design.

Plate 36. Haida fiber artist Dorothy Grant has won numerous business and design awards for her recently developed line of Haida-inspired clothing. She made this traditional-style dance blanket in 1987 out of cashmere and buttons. Its design, created by artist Robert Davidson, then Grant's husband, depicts "the Eagle giving birth to itself." Queen Charlotte Islands, British Columbia, Museum purchase. L. 139 cm. 95-25-1.

Plate 37a. This spruce-root hat was woven by Isabella Edenshaw and painted by her husband, Charles, whose "signature" has been identified as the bi-colored, four-pointed star. The crest design depicts a seal. Isabella was a highly skilled weaver and frequently twined a pattern of nested diamonds. Haida, British Columbia, ca. 1900, gift of Anne W. Meirs, 1918. Dia. 42 cm. NA8999.

Plate 37b (*top*). Detail of NA8999.

Plate 38. Umatilla Chief Peo wore this beaded deerskin jacket and matching pants on a trip to Washington to talk with U.S. Government leaders. Umatilla, Washington, collected by Stewart Culin in 1900. L. 91.5 cm. 37517.

Plate 39. Flat twined bags were made by many Plateau tribes west of the Rocky Mountains and traded to neighboring groups. Originally devised to store wild plant roots such as camus and bitterroot, they also played a role in confirming marriage ties when filled with roots and berries and given as gifts by a bride's family to that of the groom. Collected by Charles H. Stephens in 1891 from Tooth, a wife of Running Rabbit, Blackfeet. L. 62 cm. 45-15-23.

Plate 40a. This distinctive style of woman's dress was made by Plains and Plateau peoples. Its construction incorporates two complete elk skins sewn with the tail ends up which form the front and back of the dress. A third piece of hide acts as a bridge over the shoulders and beadwork covers the joining seams. Nez Perce, collected by Lieutenant M. P. Thorington when stationed at Fort Keough, Montana, 1878. L. 135 cm. 50-15-1.

Plate 40b (*above*). Detail of dress front, 50-15-1, showing elk tail.

Plate 41. Flexible baskets such as this Skokomish example are twined in a variety of techniques by native women of the Plateau region. Made most often of cattail wefts and warps overlaid with beargrass or cedar bark, they were used traditionally to store food and personal belongings. Skokomish, Washington, ca. 1900, collected by F. S. Plimpton. H. 32 cm. NA 1782.

Plate 42. At the turn of the last century, Karuk weaver Elizabeth Hickox (1872–1947) specialized in "trinket baskets." Unlike some Karuk weavers who often simplified their work for sale to tourists, Hickox consistently chose to maintain complex twining techniques. Her patron, Pasadena basketry dealer Grace Nicholson, promoted the sale of her work. Karuk, California, ca. 1910, collected by Patty S. Jewett. Dia. 18 cm. NA 8310.

Plate 43. This diagonally twined feast bowl was made ca. 1905 by Pomo weaver Sally Burris. With the influx of settlers into the central California region after 1850, native women had opportunities to make baskets for cash. The Arts and Crafts movement initiated a strong interest in basketry, and Pomo women turned this to their economic advantage, gaining prestige in both white and Indian circles. California, collected by H. K. Deisher. H. 36 cm. NA 7918.

Plate 44. Pomo weaver Sally Burris with one of her large feast bowls. Photo by H. C. Meredith, ca. 1905. Neg. S4-140400.

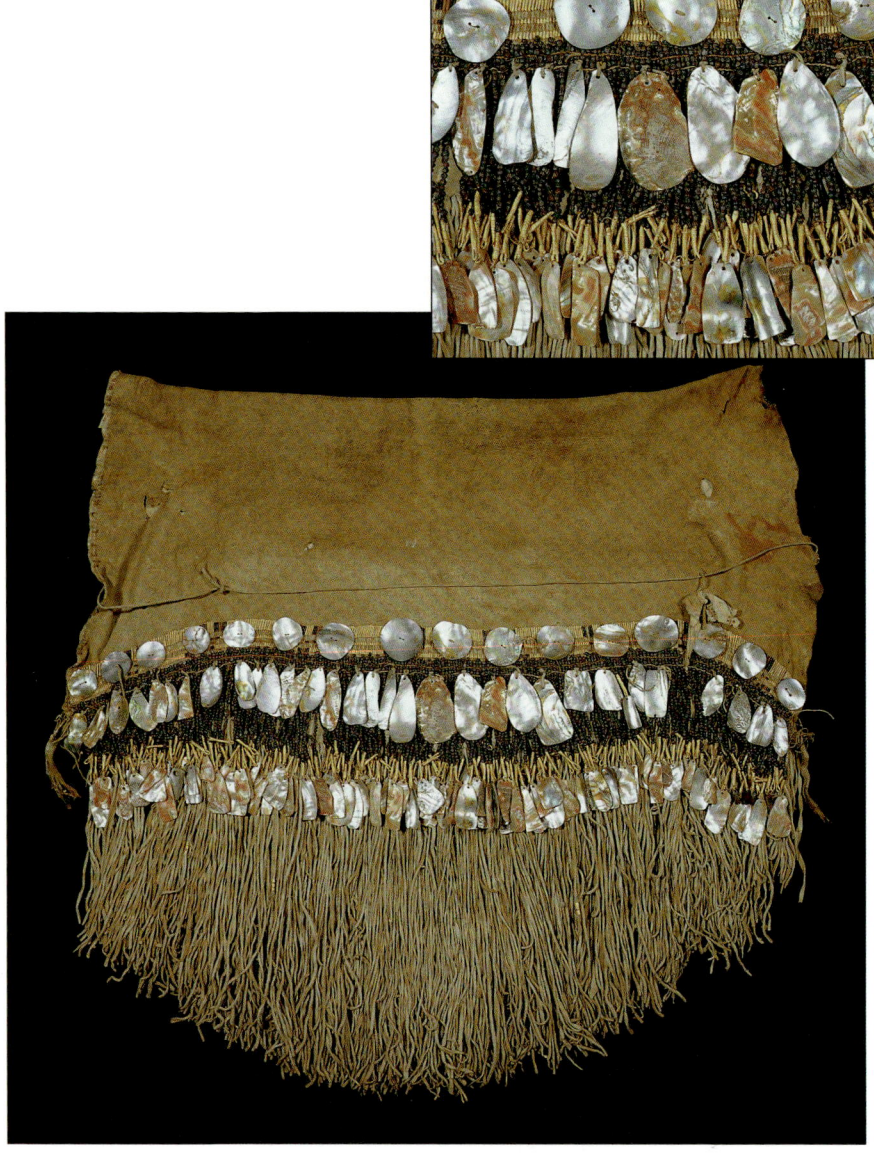

Plate 45a. Young Hupa women of northern California wear fringed buckskin dance skirts like this one on ceremonial occasions such as annual renewal rites. The skirt covers the back side of the dancer and is augmented by a narrower apron made of beargrass worn in front. The "songs" made by the fringes in motion are an important element of their use. Hupa, California, acquired from General P. H. Ray in 1915. W. 137 cm. NA 3464.

Plate 45b (*top*). Detail of Hupa dance skirt, NA3464.

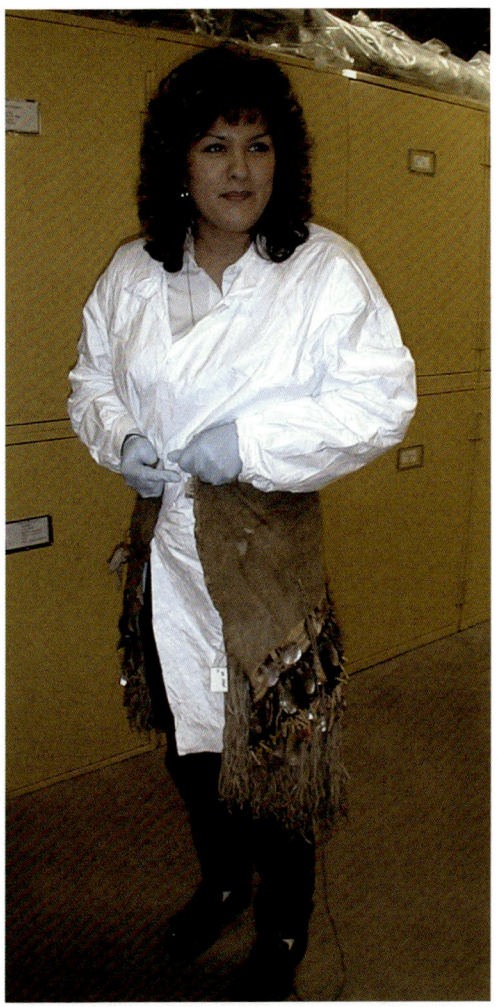

Plate 46. Shawn Kane of the Hupa Tribal Museum demonstrates for UPM staff how hide skirts are worn, 2000.

Plate 47 (*opposite, top*). Pomo women skillfully incorporate feathers into their fancy coiled gift baskets. This example includes feathers of the yellow finch and male mallard duck (green). Pomo, California, gift of Mrs. William Frishmuth, 1908. Greatest dia. 17 cm. NA 2073.

Plate 48. Native Washoe women from the California/Nevada region of Lake Tahoe traditionally made baskets in which to gather seeds, berries, roots, and nuts. Datsolalee (1850–1925), the maker of the baskets illustrated here (ca. 1910), was an especially skilled and creative weaver whose influence is visible in the work of Washoe weavers today. NA8800 (left), Dia. 34 cm, collected by Anne W. Meirs; 31-45-15 (center), Dia. 17 cm, collected by J. Brock; 38-26-1 (right), Dia. 25 cm, collected by W. Pierson.

Plate 49. From 1867 to 1880 Major John Wesley Powell studied the natives of the Colorado Plateau and Great Basin regions for the Smithsonian Institution. He amassed a large body of ethnographic and linguistic data as well as object collections at a time when they still functioned within traditional ways of life. Powell went on to become the first director of the Smithsonian's Bureau of American Ethnology. Man's shirt, Paiute, Utah, collected in 1878, Thomas Donaldson Collection. L. 51 cm. 38145.

Plate 50. This Zuni water jar was made between 1700 and 1750, when Spanish colonists actively sought to abolish local Pueblo religious and artistic forms. As a result, Pueblo material culture from this period is rare. The design depicts feathers, a theme associated with the spirit world. Ashiwi (Zuni) Polychrome, western New Mexico, collected by Jose Rafael Olguin in 1891. H. 24 cm. NA 2167.

Plate 51. This well-used water jar from Acoma Pueblo, New Mexico, was probably collected on an 1879 Bureau of American Ethnology expedition to New Mexico under the direction of Major John Wesley Powell. Acoma Polychrome, ca. 1875, gift of Frederick D. Hunt. Dia. 33 cm. 88-14-1.

Plate 52 (*top*). Made of cottonwood root, katsinas represent Hopi spirit beings who visit the villages in the spring to bring rain, good fortune, and well-being to the Hopi people. This example represents Shalako Mana and was collected in 1876 by O. D. Wheeler for John Wesley Powell. T. Donaldson Collection. H. 28 cm. 38122.

Plate 53. Stewart Culin collected numerous katsinas at Hopi and Zuni in 1901 and 1902. The Zuni Long Hair katsina (left) visits the people in the early planting season, bringing gentle rains and flowers and singing positive songs of life. Hu-tu-tu (right) represents the Zuni rain priest of the North. Zuni Pueblo, New Mexico, collected by Stewart Culin in 1902. 22616, H. 42 cm; 22615, H. 46 cm.

Plate 54. Originally taught to weave by their Pueblo neighbors, Navajo women have maintained a strong hand-weaving tradition for more than three hundred and fifty years. This wool poncho, ca. 1850, is dyed with natural indigo (blue) and with cochineal and lac (reds). It was made before the establishment of the tourist trade which dramatically altered the products woven by Navajo women. Donated by Theodore Newbold. L. 176.5 cm. 76-23-1.

Plate 55. Stewart Culin documented and collected hundreds of Native American games including this dart and ring game made of corn cobs, corn husks, and bird feathers. The game was played by boys at the Third Mesa Hopi village of Oraibi in 1901. Ring dia. 18 cm. 38615.

Plate 56. Arwen Nuttall (Four Winds Band of the Louisiana Cherokee Confederacy), Museum intern, used Culin's collection in 2002 to teach visitors about native skills and ways of learning. Nuttall's goals are to demonstrate similarities of childhood across cultures through the concepts of play and imagination and to dispel stereotypes of Native Americans.

Plate 57. Shonto Begay, a Navajo painter, author, and educator, reviewed the Museum's Navajo hide bags, horse gear, hunting equipment, and knives in 1999. His goal is to increase his students' knowledge of their ancestors and their place in the modern world.

Plate 58. Great-granddaughter of the famous Hopi potter, Nampeyo, Dextra Quotskuyva Nampeyo is a leading Pueblo artist. She uses clay dug from traditional sources near her Arizona home and coils and shapes her vessels by hand. Dextra's often innovative forms are rooted in traditional pottery styles and iconography. This jar, made in 1999, depicts birds and dragon flies. Hopi-Tewa, purchased by L. Williams. Dia. 23 cm. 99-9-2.

Plate 59. Pueblo potter Les Namingha has been inspired by artists from his mother's village of Zuni, and by his aunt, Dextra Quotskuva Nampeyo. He also studied design at Brigham Young University. The jar is entitled "Off Course" and reflects the recent development of recreational golf courses in New Mexico and Arizona. Hopi/Zuni, 1999, purchased by L. Williams. H. 13.5 cm. 99-9-6.

Plate 60. The men of New Mexico's Cochiti Pueblo have earned a reputation as makers of fine wooden double-headed drums like this one made in 1999 by Gabriel Trujillo (Yellow Bird). Drumming plays a prominent role in the renewal ceremonies held publicly at the pueblos each year and frames the performances of accompanying song and dance. Purchased by L. Williams. H. 47 cm. 99-9-1a,b.

Plate 61 (*above*). A small number of Pueblo men and women continue today to weave and embroider traditional ceremonial garments worn on ritual occasions. These textiles were made by three New Mexican women from the Tewa village of San Juan and purchased at their craft cooperative. Manta, Ramoncita Sandoval, 2001, purchased with partial funds from the Women's Committee in memory of Ruth Scott, 2001-21-1, W. 146 cm; white rain sash by Gabrielita Nave, 2002-16-1, L. 228 cm; boy's dance kilt by Pauline Cruz, 2002-16-2, L. 107 cm.

Plate 62 (*right*). Pueblo embroiderer Ramoncita Sandoval of San Juan Pueblo, New Mexico, with one of her award-winning garments in 1983.

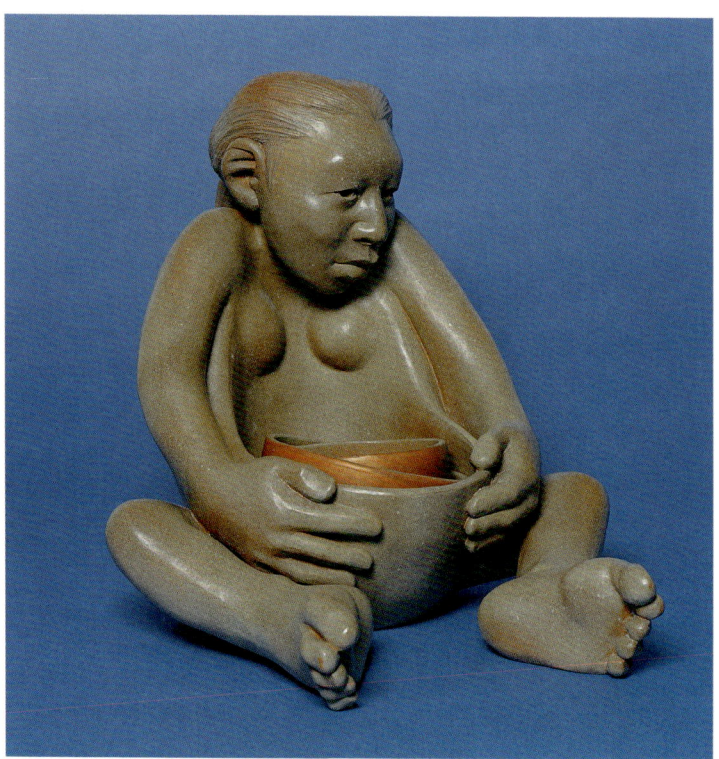

Plate 63. A provocative and internationally recognized artist from New Mexico's Santa Clara Pueblo, Roxanne Swentzell made this clay sculpture entitled "Nestled Lives" in the spring of 2000 at the time of the Los Alamos fires. "I could see the land near my home burning. When I made it, I was thinking that humans, especially women, are like vessels. Nesting bowls are seen as a sign sort of like generations—the earth holds all of us, nestled within." Purchased by L. Williams. H. 35 cm. 2000-19-1a-c.

Plate 64 (*opposite, top*). Northern Plains men of high standing wore painted buffalo robes like this one, painted by Mrs. Charging Thunder in 1882, which depicts the rising sun, the source of life and growth of all living things. Lakota, Standing Rock Reservation, South Dakota, painted in 1882, collected by James H. McLaughlin, Indian trader, 1911. L. 284 cm. NA 3985.

Plate 65 (*opposite*). In the 19th century, many northern and central Plains women wore painted buffalo robes. The geometric imagery may refer to the internal organs of the buffalo. Lakota, Standing Rock Reservation, South Dakota, painted in 1882 by Mrs. Spotted Storm Bull or Mrs. Eagleman, collected by James H. McLaughlin, 1911. L. 245 cm. NA 3989.

GUIDE TO THE NORTH AMERICAN ETHNOGRAPHIC COLLECTIONS

Plate 66. This Pawnee deerskin man's war shirt was collected in 1878, at about the time the tribe was moved from their traditional home along the North Platte River in Nebraska to the Pawnee Indian Agency, Oklahoma. Collected by Thomas Donaldson from a dealer in 1878. L. 74 cm. 37997.

Plates 67, 68 (*opposite*). This war shirt and leggings (Plate 68) exemplify the type of clothing worn by warriors on the northern plains during the early part of the 19th century. The shirt's decorative strips and the leggings' round medallions are made of bundles of horsehair wrapped in porcupine quills. Shirt, Mandan, ca. 1830, purchased by Thomas Donaldson at McIlvaine Estate sale, Philadelphia, 1885. L. 75 cm. 38251.

Plate 68a. Leggings, Mandan, ca. 1830. L. 102 cm. 38251.

Plate 68b. Detail of leggings 38251.

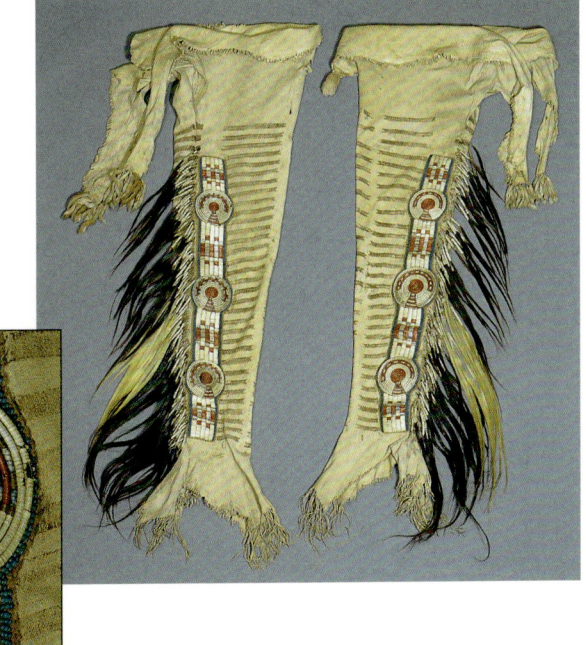

Plate 69a. This painted man's shirt made of deerskin belonged to American Horse, a late 19th century Oglala Lakota leader who advocated peace and reconciliation with the United States government. Collected before 1909 by M. A. Thompson of Fairfax, South Dakota. L. 78 cm. NA5390.

Plate 69b (*top*). Detail of shirt NA5390.

Plate 70. This characteristic Crow style man's shirt may have been owned by a pipe holder, a warrior who had led a successful war party. Crow, Montana, collected by Thomas Donaldson in 1879. L. 66 cm. 38202.

Plate 71. These Piegan Blackfeet painting tools were collected from the wife of Eagle's Rib in 1891. They include a paint bag containing red pigment, a shell paint cup, and a bone tool for applying paint. Blackfeet, Montana, Charles H. Stephens Collection. Bag, 45-15-755, W. 5.5 cm; shell cup, 45-15-752a, L. 10 cm; bone tool, 45-15-752b, L. 6 cm.

Plate 72. This early northern Plains style dress is made from a single hide sewn down one side. The fringes are wrapped with dyed porcupine quills. Northern Plains, Cree (?), ca. 1800, donated by Mrs. Edward F. Hoffman, Jr., 1912. L. 132 cm.
29-47-262.

Plate 73. Heavily beaded hide dresses became popular among Plains women during the reservation period (1865–1890). The U-shaped design at the center of the bodice is said to represent grandmother turtle on whose shell, in mythological times, mud was heaped to create the earth. The turtle is believed to give strength, longevity, and protection in childbirth. Lakota, South Dakota, collected by Brigadier General James M. Bell between 1873 and 1886. L. 139 cm. 63-3-1.

Plate 74. Deerskin dress with silver pin, Lakota, late 19th century, collected by George Gordon ca. 1915. L. 125 cm. Cg870707-8844.

Plate 75. Crow women and young girls wear dresses covered in elk teeth on important social occasions. These dresses signify the hunting prowess of a father or husband, or advertise that a female's family has sufficient wealth to acquire the items necessary to create such a dress. The teeth on this wool dress are imitation elk teeth carved of bone. Crow, Montana, collected by Ernest A. Murray in 1926. L. 84 cm. NA 10715.

Plate 76. Elk teeth symbolize long life for some Plains tribes, and babies are sometimes given a gift of an elk tooth at birth. This unusual example depicts a male elk and a porcupine. Northern Plains, collected by Charles H. Stephens. L. 3 cm. 45-15-686.

Plate 77. Some Plains tribes made umbilical cord amulets which were often tied to cradleboards or clothing and served as protective medicine throughout an individual's life. Girls' amulets were often made in the shape of a turtle, which is associated with protection. Others represent lizards, creatures that possess qualities of strength and endurance. 45-15-749 (top left) with turtle leg bones, C. H. Stephens Collection, W. 6 cm; NA 4322(top right), Standing Rock Agency, collected by Mrs. F. P. Lex, 1890, L. 14 cm; NA 5431, Lakota, collected by Mrs. M. A. Thompson before 1909, L. 16 cm.

Plate 78. A beaded umbilical amulet is attached to this child's dress made of deerskin. Southern Plains, Cheyenne/Arapaho, ca. 1890, collected by Charles H. Stephens. L. 57 cm. 45-15-266.

Plate 79. Lakota women stored dyed porcupine quills in buffalo bladder bags such as these. For some Plains tribes, porcupine quill work represented the highest attainment in women's craftsmanship, and only women of the finest character and virtue were instructed in the geometric designs. The origin of the quill society was linked to the earliest mythological beings, the buffalo. 45-15-855 (left), Charles H. Stephens Collection, 1889, L. 29 cm; NA5364 (center) Lakota, M. A. Thompson Collection, before 1909; 11750 Lakota, collected by Horatio N. Rust, 1893, L. 20 cm.

Plate 80. During the reservation period (1865–1890) pictorial imagery was increasingly incorporated into Plains women's beadwork. According to the collector, these unfinished beaded bag panels illustrate a historical event in which the Hunkpapa Lakota warrior Sitting Bull traveled to visit White Swan, a Minneconjou chief. Both men were prominent leaders in the Indian wars. Lakota, ca. 1885, collected by M. A. Thompson before 1909. NA5494 a,b.

Plate 81. Donna Shakespear-Cummings, a Northern Arapaho artist and doll maker, visited UPM in 2000 and studied the historical elements of clothing design as seen on Plains Indian dolls. Donna is shown here with her husband, Lloyd Cummings, Jr.

Plate 82. This Mandan-Hidatsa hair ornament of abalone shell, blue pony beads, and rawhide was collected by Meriwether Lewis and William Clark on their scientific exploration of 1804–1806 across what would become the western United States. Hair ornament, Mandan-Hidatsa. L. 9 cm. L-83-4.

Plate 83. This necklace, made of an eagle foot, talons, ermine tails, trade beads, and antelope dewclaws, was most likely associated with an individual's personal spirituality and guidance. North Dakota, Devil's Lake Reservation, Sisseton Dakota, ca. 1875, collected by Stuart Culin in 1900. L. 109 cm. 37676.

Plate 84. The ritual use of tobacco is common throughout much of native North America, where smoke is viewed as a means of linking earth and sky, thus providing a path to the spirit world. These pipe stems, made of wood and wrapped with porcupine quills, were collected in the 1830s by the famous American painter of native American subjects, George Catlin. Upper Missouri River, ca. 1830, Charles H. Stephens Collection. 45-15-1459 (top), L. 98 cm; 45-15-1453, L. 99 cm.

Plate 85. This stone pipe bowl, inlaid with lead and in the shape of a bear effigy, was collected in the 1830s by George Catlin. A self-taught painter from Pennsylvania, Catlin visited numerous Plains tribes and recorded what he saw in some 500 paintings and sketches. Upper Missouri River, ca. 1830, Thomas Donaldson Collection. L. 13 cm. 38377.

Plate 86. This box for storing eagle feathers was made by Powerful Cloud ca. 1852. A mnemonic inscription on the lid refers to the songs of a medicine society. North Dakota, Devil's Lake Reservation, Sisseton Dakota, collected by S. Culin in 1900. W. 45 cm. 37677.

Plate 87. This Piegan Blackfeet double-headed drum was owned by a medicine man and depicts an image of a buffalo, the most important of all Plains animals. Blackfeet, ca. 1880, collected by Thomas C. Donaldson. Dia. 40 cm. 38365.

Plate 88. Beaded shoulder sashes or baldrics were typically worn by Choctaw men in the 18th and 19th centuries. The scroll motif, also found on prehistoric Mississippian ceramics from the region, is interpreted by today's Choctaw as the giant horned serpent of southeastern mythology. Ca. 1870, collected by Stewart Culin from Earnest Fauve in Mandville, Louisiana, in 1902. 38473, L. 134 cm; 38472, L. 114 cm.

Plate 89. Earnest Fauve, Choctaw, Louisiana, wearing UPM baldrics 38472 and 38473 collected by Stewart Culin. Photo by Stewart Culin, 1902. Neg. S4-13975.

Plate 90. This Eastern Cherokee man's shirt, made of cotton muslin and decorated with partridge feathers, was collected by Frank G. Speck and John Witthoft among North Carolina's Big Cove Band between 1932 and 1940. L. 47 cm. 46-6-9.

Plate 91. Chief Will West Long wearing UPM shirt 46-6-9 and showing the appropriate manner of holding a feather wand in the Peace Dance portion of the winter Eagle Dance. Big Cove Band, Eastern Cherokee, North Carolina. Photo by Frank G. Speck, ca. 1935. Neg. S4-143939.

Plate 92. Shawnee Indian men from the region of southern Ohio wore decorated shoulder bags, an important article of male ceremonial and fancy dress among many Woodlands tribes. They were decorated with designs that represented the owner's visionary experiences or personal guardian spirits. Collected by John Clark in 1841. W. of pouch 18 cm. NA5861.

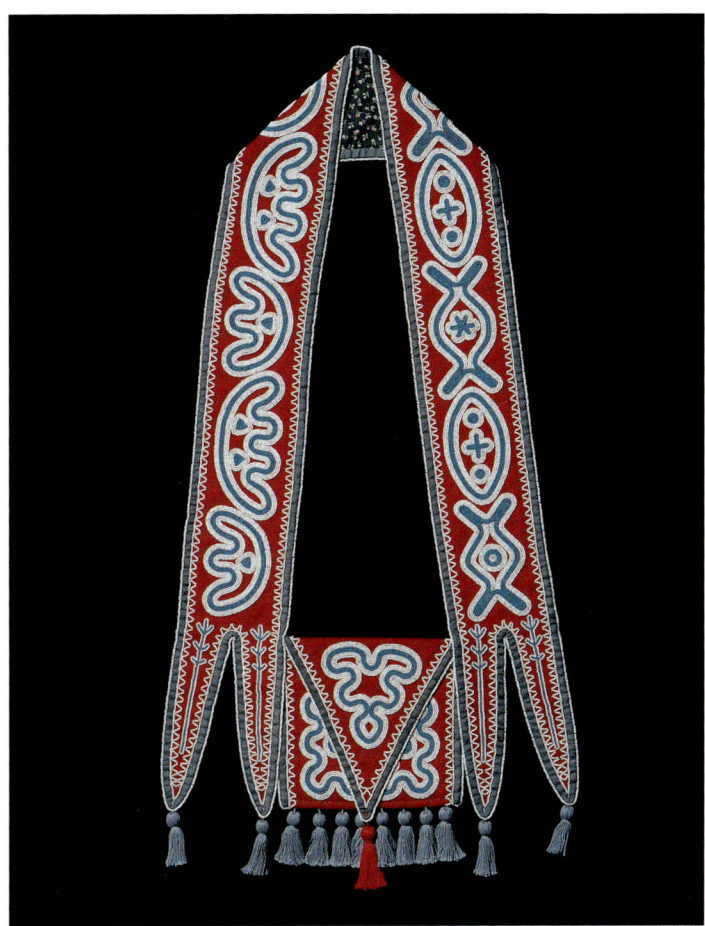

Plate 93. Contemporary Choctaw artist Jerry Ingram earned first prize at Santa Fe's 1995 Indian Market for this southeastern style man's beaded shoulder bag. Trained in commercial art and model wax carving, Ingram is self-taught in 19th century methods of Southeastern, Plateau and Northern Plains native bead, quill, and hide techniques. Museum purchase, 2002. W. of pouch approx. 18 cm. 2002-9-1.

Plate 94. Frank G. Speck and John Witthoft documented medicinal and curing practices among North Carolina's Big Cove Band of the Eastern Cherokee between 1932 and 1940. Blow tube, from medicine man Will West Long, 46-6-125, L. 23 cm; "necklace of red plum pits to prevent female ills," 46-6-37, L. 56 cm; "necklace of Job's tears, for child's teething," 46-6-139, L. 85 cm; "medicine man's skin scratchers used to strengthen ball players in advance of a game," 46-6-32, L. 8 cm, 46-6-33, L. 4 cm.

Plate 95. This wooden bowl, representing a beaver, may have been used as a feast dish. Dating to the 18th century, it was collected from members of the Kaskaskia Tribe, the then leading tribe of the Illinois confederacy. Collected by Judge George Turner in 1795. L. 48 cm. L-83-6.

Plate 96. This Shawnee man's coat is tailored of deerskin and embroidered with silk thread in the style of broad-caped coats worn by Anglo-Americans. Shawnee, St. Louis, Missouri, collected by John Clark in 1841. NA3645.

Plate 97. Women's leggings, Ojibwa (?), Great Lakes, collected by Thomas C. Donaldson at Fort Belknap, Montana, in 1891. L. 67 cm. 38208.

Plate 98 (*left*). Loom-beaded bandolier bags, styled after bags carried by British soldiers, became popular among native peoples in the areas of Wisconsin and Minnesota around 1850. They were called friendship or pony bags, and the Minnesota Ojibwa traded them regularly to the Hidatsa and Dakota for horses. Winnebago(?), Iowa, Fort Dodge, collected by Lieutenant Alfred B. Bache, 1875. L. 120 cm. 51-20-2.

Plate 99. Bandolier bag, ca. 1900, Great Lakes, collected by Anne W. Meirs, 1918. L. 159 cm. NA8694.

Plate 100. Native women of the Great Lakes region were introduced to this style of floral design from missionaries who taught them to embroider household items using silk thread. They adapted these teachings to enhance their own traditions of dress regalia using glass beads. Man's leggings, Menomini, Great Lakes, collected by M. A. Thompson before 1909. L. 71 cm. NA5389.

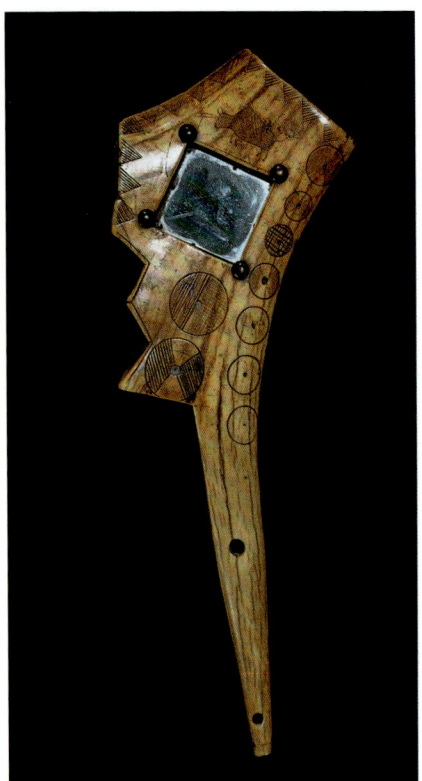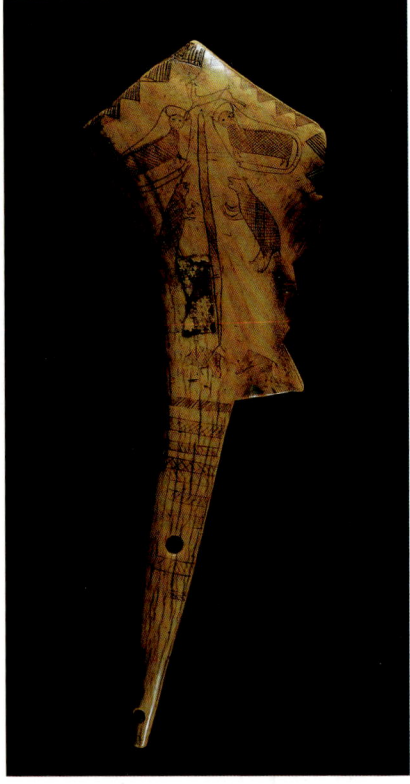

Plate 101a,b. This Winnebago ceremonial club of moose antler is incised with images of the underwater panther (the deity of the underworld), as well as badgers, buffalo, deer, and a serpent. All have lines of power emanating from their eyes. The club may have been associated with the Midewiwin or grand medicine society. Winnebago, ca. 1830, collected by Caleb Pusey. L. 34 cm. 62-15-1.

Plate 102 (*top*). Delaware women often decorated their cotton blouses with silver cut-out pins. Though the garments were Euro-American in style, the decorations reveal one way in which Woodlands women used innovative materials and styles of ornamentation to create regalia that was uniquely their own. Delaware, ca. 1850, collected by Frank G. Speck. Museum purchase. L. 54 cm. 81-24-1.

Plate 103. Unidentified Delaware woman wearing a blouse like the one shown above. Photo by George Gordon, ca. 1910. Neg. S4-143943.

Plate 104. By 1800, as the fur trade waned, Iroquois women in the region of Niagara Falls made small beaded bags for sale to tourists. Beadwork became an important source of income for Indian families. 70-9-18 (top left), S. Pennypacker Collection, W. 18 cm; 45-15-810 (top right), C. Stephens Collection, W. 16 cm; 30-1-12 (lower left), collected by Mrs. H. L. Carson, 1930, W. 16.5 cm; 38002 (lower right) Onondaga, made by the wife of Chief Daniel La Port, collected by T. Donaldson in 1900, W. 16 cm.

Plate 105. Iroquois moccasins decorated with dyed porcupine quills. Collected in 1870 and donated by Mrs. Hampton L. Carson. L. 22 cm. NA7644.

Plate 106. In the mid 19th century the Huron from the region of Quebec in central Ontario made birch-bark trays and containers embroidered with dyed moose hair for sale to tourists. 92-12-10 (top left), W. 27 cm; 92-12-11 (top right), L. 20 cm; 92-12-9 (lower right) donated by Marshall Becker in 1992, W. 21 cm; 45-15-1328 (lower left, cigarette case), Charles H. Stephens Collection, L. 13 cm.

Plate 107a (*opposite*). The game of lacrosse originated among native North American peoples, where its symbolism reveals its affinity with warfare and highlights the relationship between game and battle. For the Iroquois the game's sacred associations are linked to the seven Thunder Gods whose powers support both war and healing. Today lacrosse is still played at some villages to heal the sick. Iroquois, Cayuga, Six Nations Reserve, before 1845, collected by Frank G. Speck and donated by S. Fernberger. L. 137 cm. 53-1-17.

Plate 107b. Detail, 53-1-17.

Plate 107c. Detail, 53-1-17.

Plate 108. Mohegan carver Harold Tantaquidgeon made this mask in the 1930s, around the time Frank Speck collected it for the UPM. It is presently on long-term loan to the Tantaquidgeon Indian Museum, Uncasville, Connecticut. Bequeathed to UPM by S.W. Pennypacker. L. 25cm. 70-9-135.

Plate 109 (*above*). Beaded shoulder capes are worn by Penobscot (Maine) tribal officers. This cape was purchased from Chief Gabe Paul in 1936 and is documented in photographs as early as 1870. Its style is that of the heavy Iroquoian beadwork made after 1860. Purchased in Maine by S. Fernberger. L. 68.6 cm. 37-23-3.

Plate 110. Clara Neptune wearing UPM cape 37-23-3 (opposite page), Penobscot, Old Town Maine, 1912. Neg. S4-143944.

Appendix
Major North American Ethnographic Collections at the University of Pennsylvania Museum

REGION	CULTURE	PROVENIENCE	COLLECTOR	COLLECTION DATES
Arctic, Alaska	North Alaska Coast	Point Barrow, Wainwright, Point Belcher, Point Hope	McIlhenny, Van Valin	1897, 1917–19
Arctic, Alaska	Bering Strait Inuit, Bering Sea Inuit, Nunivak Island Inuit	Sledge Island, Diomede Island, Cape Prince of , Wales, St. Michael, King's Island, Nunivak Island	Sharp, Gordon, Hawkes, Van Valin, Rainey	1895, 1905, pre-1910, 1917–19,1950
Arctic, Alaska	Mainland SW Alaska Inuit	Kuskokwim River region	Gordon	1907
Arctic, Alaska	Pacific Inuit	Prince William Sound	de Laguna	1933
Arctic, Canada	Copper Inuit	Cockburn Point, Coppermine River, Coronation Gulf	Bernard	1915
Arctic, Canada	Iglulik	Gulf of Boothia, Fury and Hecla Strait, Repulse Bay, Wager River, Chesterfield Inlet, Southampton Island	Comer, Ford	1913, 1914
Arctic, Greenland	Greenland Eskimo	Cape York, Netchiolumi, Godhaven; Karnah-Whale Sound	Peary Relief Expedition, Peary Auxiliary Expedition	1892, 1894
Subarctic	Ingalik	Anvik, Hologochaket, middle Yukon Valley	Demoski, de Laguna	1917, 1935
Subarctic	Montagnais	Lake St. John	Speck	1931
Subarctic	Innu (Naskapi)	Labrador, Barren Ground Band	Speck	1930s
Subarctic	Chilcotin	British Columbia	Gordon	1915
Northwest Coast	Haida	Queen Charlotte Island, Masset	Culin, Newcombe, Heye	1900, 1910
Northwest Coast	Kwakwaka'wakw	Vancouver Island	Culin, Newcombe, Heye	1900, ca. 1910
Northwest Coast	Makah	Washington, Neah Bay	Culin, Heye	1900, ca. 1910
Northwest Coast	Tlingit	Alaska	Gordon, Shotridge, Emmons	1905–1932

REGION	CULTURE	PROVENIENCE	COLLECTOR	COLLECTION DATES
California	Pomo	Northern California	Culin, Dorsey, Deisher, Jewett, Meirs, Plimpton	ca. 1880–1915
California	Hupa	Northern California	Culin/Brizard, Gordon, Gist	1900, 1912, 1915
Plateau	Umatilla	Oregon	Culin	1900
Plateau	Klamath	Oregon	Culin	1900
Great Basin	Bannock	Idaho, Ft. Hall Reservation	Culin	1900
Great Basin	Eastern Shoshone	Wind River Reservation, Ft. Washakie, WY	Culin	1900
Great Basin	Ute, Uintah	Whiterocks, Utah	Nevin, Culin, Sapir, Mason	1875, 1900, 1909
Great Basin	Northern Paiute	Nevada, Pyramid Lake Reservation	Donaldson, Culin	1900
Great Basin	Paiute, Ute, Hopi		Powell	1870–88
Southwest	Pueblo, Hopi	Arizona	Donaldson, Culin, Voth, Starr	1901
Southwest	Pueblo, Zuni	New Mexico	Culin, Cushing	1902
Plains	Arapaho	Wind River Reservation, WY	Culin, Gottschall	1900, 1871–1909
Plains	S. Arapaho/ S. Cheyenne	Darlington Agency, OK	Starr, Gottschall	1893, 1931
Plains	Blackfeet	Montana	Stephens	1891
Plains	Crow	Montana	Murray	1926
Plains	Western and Eastern Sioux	Fort Peck Reservation, MT; Devil's Lake Reservation, ND; Pine Ridge Agency, SD	Culin, Frazier, Gottschall, Thompson, Stephens	1900, 1911, 1939
Plains	Plains	Upper Missouri River region	Catlin	1830s
Southeast	Cherokee, Eastern Band	North Carolina	Speck, Witthoft	1932–40
Northeast	Algonquin	Quebec, River Desert Band	Johnson	1929
Northeast	Penobscot	Maine	Fernberger	1933
Northeast	Iroquois, Cayuga	Ontario, Six Nations Reserve, Grand River	Pennypacker, Culin	ca. 1900
Northeast	Delaware	Oklahoma; Ontario, Grand River	Pennypacker	ca. 1900
Northeast	Ottawa	Michigan	Gottschall	1871–1909
Northeast	Chippewa-Ojibwa	Minnesota	Gottschall	1871–1909

REGION	CULTURE	PROVENIENCE	COLLECTOR	COLLECTION DATES
Inter-regional	All regions with emphasis in the West	Philadelphia collector, Special Agent in charge of 11th US Census survey on conditions of Native Americans, 1890, purchased directly from natives and dealers	Donaldson	ca. 1870–98
Inter-regional	All regions with particular interest in Native American games	Early UPM Curator of General Ethnology, conducted three collecting expeditions	Culin	1899–1902
Inter-regional	Arapaho (OK), Cheyenne (OK), Chippewa, Makah, Nootka, Ottawa, Pueblo, Quinault, Sioux (SD)	Pennsylvania printer, itinerant trader and collector, acquired objects directly from native groups	Gottschall	1871–1909
Inter-regional	All regions with emphasis on Blackfeet, Plains and Southwestern groups	Pennsylvania illustrator and collector, acquired objects directly from natives and through dealers	Stephens	ca. 1880–1910
Inter-regional	Primarily Northwest Coast, eastern Plains, and Great Lakes regions	New York collector, acquired objects directly from natives and through dealers	Heye	ca. 1895–1918
Inter-regional	All regions with emphasis on Northeast and Plains	Pennsylvania resident, student of Speck, acquired collections primarily from Speck and natives and through dealers	Pennypacker	ca. 1930–1950

Index

Numbers in **bold** refer to illustration plates

Abbott, Charles C. xi, 3
Academy of Natural Sciences of Philadelphia xiii, 5
Acoma Polychrome **51**
Acoma Pueblo **51**
Ahtna **13**
Alaska Native Brotherhood 13
Algonquin 5, 13, 14, 93, **31**
American Horse 17, **69**
amulets 6, **77, 78**
animal imagery 6
anthropology 3
Apache 5
Arapaho 5, 6, 93, 94, **78, 81**
Arctic 1, 4, 5, 6, 10, 16, 92, **1–9**
Ashiwi Polychrome **50**
Athapaskan 6, 10, **9, 10, 12, 13**
atigi **8**
atigluk **7**
Avery Island. *See* McIlhenny

bags 6, 9, 15, 16, **16, 39, 71, 79, 92, 93, 98, 99, 104**
baskets 7, 10, 11, 12, 14, **41–43, 47, 48**
beadwork 1, 15, **8, 16, 19, 20, 38, 40, 66, 69, 70, 73, 74, 78, 80, 88, 92, 93, 98–100, 104, 109**
bears 2, 12, 14, **18, 23, 25, 26, 31, 85**
beavers 14, **34, 95**
Begay, Shonto 57
Bella Bella 11
Bering Sea Eskimo 8, 10, 92
Bering Strait Eskimo 4, 10, 92
Bernard, Captain Joseph 10, **2**
birds 5, 6, **3–5**, 10, **24, 36, 47, 55, 58, 83, 86, 90**
Blackfeet 5, 93, 94, **39, 71, 87**
Boas, Franz 3, 10, 12, 14
Brinton, Daniel G. xi, 3
Brizard 93
buffalo 2, **64, 65, 79, 87, 101**

Bureau of Indian Affairs 7
Burris, Sally **43, 44**

Catlin, George 2, 93, **84, 85**
Cayuga. *See* Iroquois
Cherokee 5, 13, 14, 16, 93, **56, 90, 91, 94**
Cheyenne 5, 93, 94, **78**
Chilcotin 92, **14**
Choctaw 16, **88, 89**, 93
Clark, William 2, **32, 82**
clothing 3, 5, 6, 9, 10, 12, 15, **5–9, 12, 13, 15, 19, 26, 27, 36–38, 40, 45, 49, 54, 61, 64–70, 72–75, 78, 88, 90, 92, 93, 96, 97, 100, 102, 105, 109**
Cochiti Pueblo **60**
Comer, Captain George 10, **8**
Copper Eskimo 4, 10, 92
Cree **19, 20, 72**
Crow 5, 93, **70, 75**
Culin, Stewart xi, 6, 7, 8, 16, 17, 18, 92–94, **38, 53, 55, 56, 83, 86, 88, 89**
Cushing, Frank Hamilton xi, 2, 7, 8, 93

Dakota **83, 86**
Datsolalee **48**
de Laguna, Frederica 2, 92, **13, 29**
Deisher, Henry 10, 93, **43**
Delaware 11, 93, **102, 103**
Demoski, Leo 92, **11**
divination **18**
Donaldson, Thomas C. 2, 93, **49, 52, 66–68, 70, 85, 87, 97, 104**
Dorsey, George 6, 93
dreams 2, 14, 15, **16**
drums **60, 87**
Dutchman, Raymond xiii, 16, **10**

eagle **22, 24, 36, 83, 86, 91**
Edenshaw, Charles and Isabella **37**
elk **12, 40, 75, 76**
elk teeth **75, 76**

Emmons, George T. 10, 92, **31**
Era **8**

Fauve, Earnest **89**
Fernberger, Samuel 14, 93, **107**, **109**
Fielding, Fidelia 14
fishing equipment 3, 5, 10, 11, 12
Ford, Henry 10, 92
Frazier, William W. 93

games 3, 6, 7, 8, 16, **55**, **56**, **94**, **107**
Gist, Frank 10, 93
Gordon, George B. iv, xi, 3, 8–13 (Figs. 5, 6), 17, 92, 93, **4–6**, **9**, **12**, **14**, **21**, **74**, **103**
Gottschall, Amos H. 93, 94
Grant, Dorothy **36**

Haida 11, 92, **30**, **32**, **34–37**
hats 1, 12, 13, 15, **22**, **23**, **37**
Hawkes, E. W. 92
Heye, George G. 2, 10, 11, 92, 94, **30**
Hickox, Elizabeth **42**
Holikachuk 4, **11**
Hopi xi, 2, 7, 16, 18, 93, **52**, **55**, **58**, **59**
hunting equipment 1, 3, 5, 10, 12, **1–3**, **15–17**, **57**
Hupa 4, 6, 93, **45**, **46**
Huron **106**

Iglulik 10, **8**
Ingalik 4, 92, **10**, **11**
Ingram, Jerry 16, **93**
Innu iv, 2, 4, 13, 14, 15, 17, 92, **15–18**
Inuit 1, 2, 4, 6, 8, 9, 92
Iñupiaq 5, 6, **2**, **3**, **7**
Iroquois 5, 13, 14, 93, **104**, **105**, **107**
Isleta Pueblo 7

Jewett, Patty S. 93, **42**
Johnson, Frederick 5, 93

Kane, Shawn **46**
Karuk **42**
Kaskaskia **95**
katsinas 7, **52**, **53**
Klukwan, Alaska xii, 9, 11, 12, **21**, **23**, **25**
knowledge 2
Kwakwaka'wakw 10, 92, **30**

lacrosse **107**
Lakota 1, 5, 6, 10, 11, 17, **64**, **65**, **69**, **73**, **74**, **77**, **79**, **80**
Lewis, Meriwether 2, **82**
longevity **73**

Mandan **67**, **68**, **82**
masks 5, 6, 12, 16, **1**, **10**, **11**, **30**, **32**, **108**
Mason, J. Alden 93
material culture, meaning of 1, 6, 17
McIlhenny, Edward Avery xi, xiii, 2, 5, 6, 8, 17, 92, **3**
medicines 3, **77**, **86**, **87**, **94**
Meirs, Anne W. 93, **37**, **48**, **99**
Menomini **100**
moccasins **9**, **105**
Mohegan 14, 16, **108**
Murray, E. A. 93, **75**

NAGPRA 15, 16
Namingha, Les **59**
Nampeyo, Dextra Quotskuyva **58**, **59**
Naskapi. *See* Innu
National Museum of the American Indian's artist-in-residence program 16
Native American Graves Protection and Repatriation Act. *See* NAGPRA
Native Hawaiians 15
natural history, early links with anthropology 2
Navajo 5, 16, 18, 91, **54**, **57**
Neptune, Clara **110**
Nevin, William N. 93
Newcomb, C. F. 92
Nez Perce **40**
Nicholson, Grace **42**
Northwest Coast natives 11, 12, 92, 94, **21–32**, **34–37**
Nunivak Island 4, 9, 92
Nuttall, Arwen xiii, 16, **56**
Nuu-cha-nulth 11
Nuxalt **33**

Ojibwa 93, **97**, **98**
Onondaga **104**
Orchard, W. C. 11
Osage xi, 10, 11

Paiute xi, 4, 6, 93, **49**
Pawnee **66**
Peary Auxiliary Expedition 92
Peary Relief Expedition 92
Pennypacker, S. W. 93, **104**, **108**
Penobscot **109**, **110**
Peo, Chief **38**
Pepper, William 5
Pequot 14
Philadelphia Centennial Exposition of 1876 3
philosophy, Native American 2

pipes 3, **84**, **85**
Plains tribes **64–66**, **70–72**, **75–81**, **83**, **85–87**
Plateau tribes **38–41**
Plimpton, F. S. 10, 93, **41**
Pomo 4, 93, **43**, **44**, 47
porcupine quills **9**, **12**, **62**, **67, 68**, **72**, **79**, **84**, **105**
pottery 3, 7, **50**, **51**, **58**, **59**, 63
Powell, John Wesley 2, 93, **49**, **51**, **52**
Powerful Cloud **86**
Pueblo xiii, 5, 7-8 (Fig. 4), 16, 91, 93, 94, **50–53**, **55**, **58-63**

Rainey, F. 92
reciprocity 14
renewal 2, 8, **45**, **60**
ritual items 3, 7, 9, **45**, **52**, **53**, **61**, **92**, **101**, **107**

San Juan Pueblo **61**, **62**
Sandoval, Ramoncita **61**, **62**
Santa Clara Pueblo **63**
Sapir, Edward 93
Saunders, Silas Art **33**
seals **2**, **5**, **30**, **37**
Sebbelov, Gerda 10
Shakespear-Cummings, Donna **81**
Sharp, B. 92
Shawnee **92**, **96**
Shoshone 6, 93
Shotridge, Louis iv, xi, xii, 2, 4, 11 (Fig. 7), 12, 13, 17, 18, 92, **22-28**
Sitting Bull **80**
Skokomish **41**
Smithsonian Institution 7, 10, **49**
Speck, Frank G. iv, xi, 3, 5, 11, 13, 14, 15, 16, 17, 18, 92, 93, 94, **15–19**, **90**, **91**, **94**, **102**, **107**, **108**
Starr, F. 93

Stephens, Charles H. 93, **32**, **39**, **71**, **76–79**, **84**, **104**, **106**
Subarctic **10–20**
Swentzell, Roxanne **63**

Tantaquidgeon Indian Museum **108**
Tantaquidgeon, Gladys 16
Tantaquidgeon, Harold **108**
Tewa **58**, **61–63**
textiles 7, **35**, **36**, **39**, **54**, **61**
Thompson, Mary A. 10, **69**, **77**, **79**, **80**, **100**
Tlingit xi, xii, 1, 4, 9, 10, 11, 12, 13, 17, 18, 92, **21–29**, **31**
tourist trade 11, **30**, **42**, **43**, **54**, **104**, **106**
trade goods 2, **39**, **83**, **98**, **99**
Trujillo, Gabriel **60**
tunghat 6
turtle **73**, 77

Umatilla 4, 6, 93, **38**
umbilical amulet **77**, **78**
University of Pennsylvania Museum 1, 3

Vanderhoop, Evelyn **35**
Van Valin, William B. 10, 92
"vanishing" Indian 2, 3
Voth, H. R. 93

Wanamaker, John 11
Washoe **48**
West Long, Chief Will **91**, **94**
White Swan **80**
Winnebago iv, **98**, **101**
Witthoft, John 5, 14, 93, **90**, **94**

Yuchi 14
Yup'ik **1**, **2**, **4–6**

Zuni ball game 8
Zuni Pueblo 7, 8, **50**, **53**, **59**

About the Author

Lucy Fowler Williams is Keeper of American Section Collections at the University of Pennsylvania Museum of Archaeology and Anthropology. She is co-author with Joe Ben Wheat of the 1994 exhibition catalogue *A Burst of Brilliance: Germantown, Pennsylvania and Navajo Weaving,* and is currently pursuing dissertation research on Pueblo textiles.